INSTALLING
RADIO CONTROL
IN BOATS

Other titles in this series include:

Installing Radio Control Equipment   Peter Smoothy
Building From Plans   David Boddington
Setting Up Radio Control Helicopters   Dave Day
Basic Radio Control Flying   David Boddington
Flying Scale Gliders   Chas Gardiner
Moulding and Glassfibre Techniques   Peter Holland
Operating Radio Control Engines   Brian Winch & David Boddington
Covering Model Aircraft   Ian Peacock
Radio Control Vintage Model Aeroplanes   Peter Russell
Flying Radio Control Gliders   George Stringwell
Scale Model Airplanes   David Boddington
Learning to Fly Radio Control Helicopters   Dave Day
Flying Radio Control Aerobatics   Charles Allison & Andy Nicholls
Engines for Ducted Fans   David James
Radio Control Scale Boats   John Cundell

Installing Radio Control In Boats

John Cundell

ARGUS BOOKS

Argus Books

Argus House
Boundary Way
Hemel Hempstead
Hertfordshire HP2 7ST
England

First published by Argus Books 1990

© Argus Books 1990

ISBN 1 85486 022 4

Phototypesetting by GCS, Leighton Buzzard
Printed and bound in Great Britain by
William Clowes Ltd., Beccles

Contents

Introduction

MOST PEOPLE can build a model boat that will probably float and move around on the water. Most people can also install radio control equipment in that model and enjoy a reasonable amount of control over it. But, like all things in life that require a modicum of technical ability, there is always a better way of going about things which will inevitably result in better performance, reliability, satisfaction and more enjoyment, rather than the frustration and perhaps ultimate loss of interest that can result from a 'slapdash' approach.

Now I am not saying that this is the 'bible' for R/C installations in model boats – far from it! – but application of some of the principles and ideas included in this book will no doubt improve your model's performance, solve some problems, definitely save you some time, and perhaps even some money.

Chapter 1
What is Radio Control?

RADIO CONTROL of models was beyond belief not fifty years ago. Before the Second World War all model boats were free running, apart from round the pole tethered hydroplanes!

The first radio control equipment was most definitely for radio enthusiast operation rather than a modeller's. The sets were large, the batteries enormous; reliability was non-existent and you needed a craft so large that it approached the real thing rather than a scale model. How different things are today. Even the man in the street is aware of the immense strides that have been made in telecommunications – for instance, television in the home direct from satellites and the ability to radio control a spacecraft at and beyond the extreme edge of the Solar System. Radio control of models hasn't quite reached that stage yet, but the spin-off from high technology and large scale production, particularly in Japan, has brought the cost of fully proportional, multi-channel equipment well within the buying power of every modeller, and with a degree of reliability and performance undreamed of in those early days. Today we can buy radio control outfits for under £50 which will fit easily into a 16"-long model – even smaller if a little ingenuity is applied. Radio technology is a part of everyday existence. We all use it without a second thought as to how it works. The aim of this book is not to baffle you with science, but to provide you with basic and practical information in choosing, installing and operating the wonders of the black box.

Early Days

There is a recorded example of radio control as early as the beginning of this century when, in 1905, a Professor Branly demonstrated remote operation of machinery for an industrial requirement and in the early 1920s a model airship was supposedly controlled by radio during a music hall performance.

There is some disagreement as to the first use of R/C in a boat. However, there is a documented case at the north end of Lake Windermere in 1920 when R/C experiments with the recently restored full-size powerboat, *White Lady*, took place using a spark generation system. An electrical spark releases a surge of energy into the ether, causing a short radio emission over a wide band of frequencies (some readers will recall early television days when cars were not fitted with spark interference suppressors, causing reception difficulties). It is fairly simple to detect this emission and for the receiving apparatus to switch a circuit.

R/C in models started in the USA in the 1930s, particularly for model aircraft use. There was no commercial development and R/C remained the province of the radio amateur experimenter, and things stayed this way right through the war years and into the 1950s. There was a little development in the late 1940s, again particularly with model engines, and one or two manufacturers realised there was a potential market for model boats and produced a maritime range of fittings. One such company was Ripmax – now the distributors of perhaps the world's best known range of R/C equipment, Futaba.

The first R/C model boat event was at Blackpool in August 1952 and was for boats fitted with rudder control only. At the Poole club's event in September of that year, one of the pioneers of British R/C equipment, George Honnest-Redlich, was a competitor. George had made a name for himself in 1951 by successfully crossing the Channel with a small diesel powered launch under R/C from a three function tuned reed outfit.

This latter system was the first truly multi-channel equipment – that is the ability to operate more than one discipline on a particular model. Before that, only single channel was available, limited to the rudder on a boat unless one was prepared to descend into the world of special electro/mechanical sequence devices which could simulate

multi-channel use. These were very fussy and notoriously unreliable.

Tone systems worked by transmitting a low frequency audio tone to the receiver. Each switch or button on the transmitter would send a tone at a different frequency. The receiver didn't attempt to separate the tones electronically, but sent them to a bank of small metal reeds cut to different lengths. Like the tuning fork on a piano these would only vibrate at a certain frequency governed by their length. The reeds were allowed to vibrate against a minute contact and this electrical signal pulled in a relay which was wired to the respective switch or servo. The equipment did not develop all that quickly and it was 1958 before six-channel gear became commonly available. Then, the cost of a six-channel outfit, just transmitter and receiver was £70; in today's terms, approximately £500! Despite these improvements, the number of users was still relatively small as the modeller was still required to carry out a considerable amount of installation work, in particular wiring the equipment into the model, and because only one set of R/C gear could be switched on at any one time.

A breakthrough came in the early 1960s when super-heterodyne circuits appeared; these were more selective and could allow two models to operate at the same time. This allowed events where two boats could be raced together following careful tuning of the R/C gear, and a number of knockout competitions were held, but often the most exciting part of the day, the final between the two fastest boats, could not be held because of radio interference. However, it wasn't long before true multi-radio equipment arrived, and at last, reliable, competitive events could be organised with models and modellers competing against one another rather than against the clock.

Early Days! A home-made transmitter – there were no other kind – built as a ship's control dais complete with steering wheel and throttle lever, *circa* 1950.

The last major development was proportional control at the end of the 1960s, and the R/C set as we know it today had finally arrived.

Today's Standards

All R/C sets sold today are fully proportional. This means that the movement of a control surface on the model is exactly proportional to the amount of movement imparted to the transmitter stick. This demands a much more complex method of signalling and could only come about with the advent of the transistor.

Latterly, the microprocessor chip has brought the world of the computer into R/C systems, and it is now possible to purchase equipment which can be taught a series of operations, and these subsequently 'played' back by the transmitter on demand; particularly useful for some of the complicated movement sequences required when flying model aircraft, especially helicopters. And, of course, this ultra-sophisticated equipment is ultra-expensive.

However, mass production, particularly by the Japanese, has brought prices down to very acceptable standards in terms of reliability and price. R/C gear is now regarded as a tool or a means to an end rather than a tinkerer's delight.

Transmitter

These are hand-held and come in a variety of shapes, sizes and colours, and they are the part of the R/C system most susceptible to cosmetic sales appeal and ergonomic design. The almost universal material of construction is plastic, although a small number of specialist manufacturers still custom make in metal. The size is usually that of a medium-sized book, and it will have a control knob, a steering wheel or much more likely, a number of levers or 'sticks'. Inside the transmitter these are connected to variable resistances which control the amount of current or voltage going to each electronic circuit. The sticks have small levers underneath or alongside known as 'trims'. These are used for minute setting-up adjustments and will be described in more detail later. The number of sticks depends upon the number of operational channels or functions that the system is designed to handle.

There will also be an on-off switch and usually a needle meter giving an indication of battery voltage and/or signal strength. Most of the lower end range sets are powered with dry cells, usually pencells, and there will be an access hatch for changing these. If

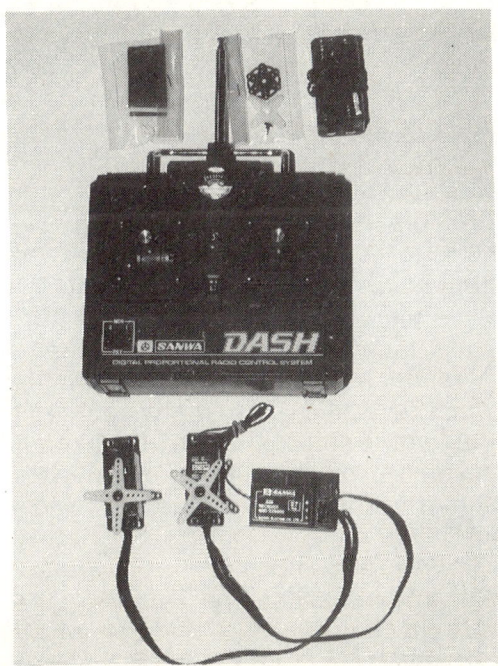

Modern proportional two function system; reliable, good value for money. At top, frequency pennant, spare servo discs and receiver battery box; at bottom, two servos and receiver.

rechargeable nickel cadmium cells can be fitted, then a charging socket will be included.

There will be a telescopic aerial which, when extended, radiates the signal whose field somewhat resembles that of a gigantic doughnut. The aerial is at the centre of this doughnut and is least effective when aimed directly at the model – one should always try and align the transmitter aerial parallel to the receiver aerial. The range of the transmitted signal is about 1½ miles maximum, but most operators become disoriented at distances over 200 yards so there should be ample signal strength to spare.

There will also be a socket for the transmitter crystal which, in conjunction with its matching crystal in the receiver, determines which frequency the set is operating on. Always make sure you have the transmitter crystal in the transmitter and the receiver crystal in

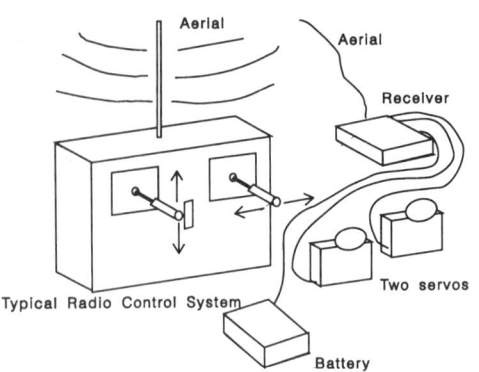

Typical Radio Control System

the receiver. Incorrect positioning will result in a very weak signal.

Even the bottom of the range sets now have servo reversing switches. These are simple two way switches which determine the way the servo will travel when the stick is operated – either clockwise or anti-clockwise; very useful for setting up a difficult installation and when swapping receiver from model to model. Without this facility it is necessary to carefully check installation locations for servos and perhaps even purchase 'opposite' handed servos for difficult problems. In my opinion, servo reversing switches are a must and worth paying the few pounds extra.

Middle and top of the range sets increase in sophistication and the number of functions, culminating in a drop-down panel on the transmitter which allows individual adjustment of servo centre positions, rate switches which determine how many degrees of rotation the servo will turn for maximum movement of the stick, programmable memories for special sequences, and so on.

Finally, a number of outfits are sold with a modular facility. This is a small 'cockpit' usually at the back of the transmitter, in which a suitably shaped electronic box can be inserted. This box determines the frequency band of the R/C equipment; either 27MHz, 35MHz or

Back of transmitter case showing lid at bottom over battery compartment and crystal cover at right. Sticker at left shows where nicad charging jack socket point can be fitted at a later date.

40MHz. Such a facility is useful if you intend to fly model aircraft as well as boats and cars as by law there are specific legal frequency bands which must be adhered to for specific categories of models. I shall look at these frequency allocations later.

Receiver

A typical receiver will measure approximately 2½"×1½"×1", and again is usually of plastic construction. A row of sockets at one end takes the servo plugs and a power supply plug from the receiver batteries. There will be a small access hole, usually protected by a push-in rubber plug, under which will be found the matching frequency crystal. Receivers normally operate at one frequency band, ie. 27MHz, 35MHz or 40MHz; if a modular facility is provided on the transmitter, then the receiver will have a similar facility whereby modular units on the other frequency bands can be purchased if necessary.

A length of wire, approximately 18" long, emerges from the receiver case, and this is the aerial. It must not be shortened in its overall length during installation. The power supply harness usually includes an on-off switch. BEC systems, which I discuss in Chapter 6, do not require the switch harness.

Close up of receiver showing exchangeable crystal under removed cap. Top right hand socket is for battery input; other two for servos.

Servos

These are miniature electro-mechanical units about the size of a matchbox, each containing a small precision electric motor which drives an output shaft through an efficient gear train. The case is again of plastic, as are the gears. The reduction ratio is about 1:20 which will develop several pounds of pull at the servo disc, and has a rotary movement of about 90 degrees, which can be adjusted from transmitters equipped with rate switches.

When the servo receives a signal from the transmitter/receiver the motor turns, which rotates the output disc via

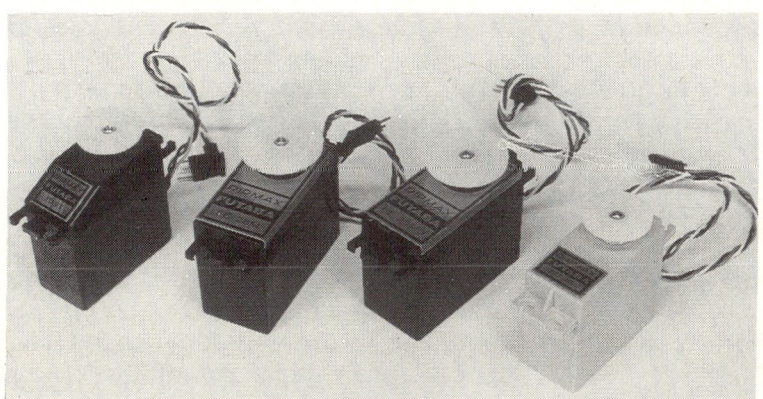

Four slightly different servos. Basically only the packaging is different; they all do the same job quite adequately.

the gearbox. Attached to the servo output disc shaft within the case is a variable resistance. The electronic circuitry within the servo monitors the output from this resistance against the incoming signal until an electronic balance is achieved and no further voltage is applied to the motor, so the rotation of the disc ceases, and is maintained until the transmitter stick is once again moved, when the whole balancing process starts again. Hence, as you move the stick a small amount, the servo output disc moves a corresponding amount – proportional control.

Winches

Model yachts require a special type of servo to operate the sails. These 'beefed-up' units usually employ larger motors and much stronger gear trains, and the output shaft drives a drum approximately 1"–1½" in diameter. Whereas the servo only moves its output disc through approximately 45 degrees in any one direction, the winch will turn its drum a number of revolutions. The 'sheets' or cords attached to the sails are wound around the drum and, by rotating one way or the other, the sheets can be wound out or in and consequently the sails let in or out. The pressure on a sail sheet can be in tens of pounds, hence the winch must be strong enough to handle this, and still operate fast enough to wind the sheets in and out as quickly as possible, as required in racing conditions. Quite often the drum will be split into two parts of different diameters, giving different winding speeds for the main and jib sails.

Because of the heavy power demand, winches usually have a separate and larger battery pack than feeds the receiver.

A typical sail winch, this one with different diameter drums. Usually the drums are mounted axially above one another on the same side of the winch.

Frequencies

Various parts of the radio spectrum, and that includes television which is simply a complicated radio signal, are assigned for users by the governing authorities, in the case of Great Britain by the Department of Trade and Industry. The part of the band given over for radio control users is restricted to different ranges in different countries. However, the almost universal range is 26.96 to 27.28MHz. Within the United Kingdom's allocated band, it is possible to operate twelve different models at one and the same time on different frequencies or 'slots' as they are known.

Although in America and some parts of Europe the band has suffered at the hands of Citizens Band enthusiasts, particularly for model aircraft operation where interference is more liable and usually much more catastrophic than with a boat model, the authorities in this country, despite a period of chaos and confusion in the early unlicensed days of CB, have resisted infiltration on

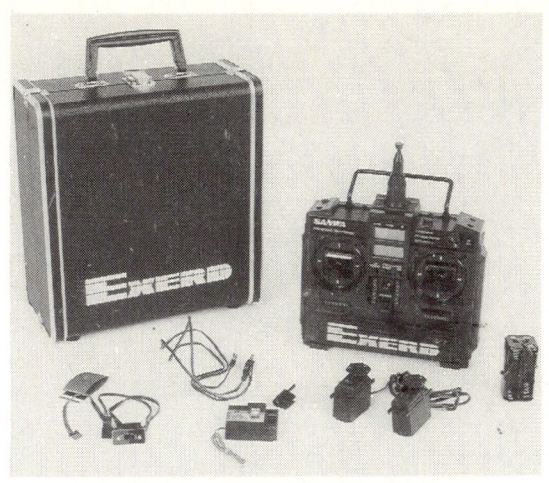

The latest in two channel equipment on 40MHz; incorporates electronic trimmers for positioning all aspects of servo or speed controller and a stopwatch for timing races, battery charging, etc. Cost is approximately five times that of the simple two function equipment.

27MHz AM. CB channels are allocated part of the 27MHz FM band, on slightly different frequencies to those in general use by modellers. Experience has shown that there is little if any interference caused to radio control users.

Most causes of control loss are not caused by interference, but nearly always by badly maintained or faulty equipment. There will always be those who operate illegal equipment but, if your radio gear is correctly aligned, relatively little if any trouble is to be experienced on 27MHz.

There are three other bands in Great Britain also allocated to radio control – 35MHz, 40MHz and 459MHz, the latter sometimes known as Ultra High Frequency (UHF). The former has been provided solely for model aircraft operation and this is a legal requirement. If your supplier tells you that 35MHz can be used in your area, he is inciting you to break the law. Because of this fact, your local club, being law-abiding members of the National Association, will not allow the frequency to be used on their water.

Negotiations with the Department recently succeeded in the allocation of the 40MHz frequency for surface vehicle users – boats and cars – and there are thirty slots available. 40 MHz is legally restricted to surface vehicle use; aircraft users are breaking the law. Sets in this band are now generally available at a higher price than 27 MHz equipment due to the higher specification. However, 27 MHz is still by far and away the predominant band used by model boat enthusiasts and is likely to remain the major radio control frequency for many years.

As far as the UHF band is concerned, the comparative electronic sophistication required to make use of this band resulted in high prices. I say 'resulted' as, at the time of writing, there is no company currently manufacturing equipment on this frequency, despite a number of attempts in the past.

I stated earlier the frequency band within which the 27 MHz allocation is allowed is 26.960 to 27.280 MHz. This band can be proportionally divided to allow for twelve sets of radio equipment to be operated simultaneously without interfering with each other. The miniature metal case houses a specially ground piece of quartz crystal, which will vibrate at only one specific frequency determined by the shape when subjected to an electric current.

In order to make it easy to identify the frequency in use for personal and other modellers' benefit – remember only one frequency can be operated at one and the same time, otherwise severe interference will result – it has been agreed in the United Kingdom that each 27 MHz transmitter should carry a flag or pennant of certain colours. The six 'solid' colours, sometimes also known as 'spots', were the maximum number of frequencies that could be simultaneously operated when crystal controlled equipment first appeared, but most equipment sold today can successfully operate on closer frequency tolerances, although difficulties can still occur when operating with older gear that was not designed for such precise use. The later seven frequencies were fitted in between the 'solids' and came to be known as 'splits'. It is important to understand that the transmitter and receiver crystals are not the same frequency, which is why it is important not to get them muddled up.

40 MHz transmitters also carry a flag which is of one colour, green, but which has the frequency number shown to differentiate from other users. The recommendations are shown in the table.

Transmitter MHz	Colour
26.975	grey/brown
26.995	brown
27.025	brown/red
27.045	red
27.075	red/orange
27.095	orange
27.125	orange/yellow
27.145	yellow
27.175	yellow/green
27.195	green
27.225	green/blue
27.255	blue

Transmitter MHz	Number
40.665	665
40.675	675
40.685	685
40.695	695
40.705	705
40.715	715
40.725	725
40.735	735
40.745	745
40.755	755
40.765	765
40.775	775
40.785	785
40.795	795
40.805	805
40.815	815
40.825	825
40.835	835
40.845	845
40.855	855
40.865	865
40.875	875
40.885	885
40.895	895
40.905	905
40.915	915
40.925	925
40.935	935
40.945	945
40.955	955

When first purchased, your crystals will either be in small plastic holders or wrapped with a plastic sleeve to identify them. If these identifiers become lost or damaged, you will note that the metal crystal cases have their frequency stamped on them. From reading the above, some modellers may consider that surely it is just a simple case of using 35 or 40 MHz band crystals in 27 MHz band equipment and vice versa. Unfortunately, the large difference between the frequency bands means that different component values have to be used in the receiver and transmitter circuits, and the equipment will not function at all if this modification is attempted. And, please remember, any person who informs you that 35 MHz can be used for model boats is inciting you to break the law. 35 MHz is only for aircraft, as 40 MHz is only for boats and cars. The penalty is confiscation of your equipment, a £2,000 find and/or three months in prison!

Mode

Mode means method of control, and in this respect applies to the layout of the sticks on the transmitter. Most two-function equipment will have the throttle on the left in a vertical mode, with the rudder as a horizontal mode on the right. In some cases, the rudder stick is replaced by a steering wheel (purely a matter of personal choice) – try a 'dry run' at the model shop before purchase, or better still try and get your hands on someone else's equipment before finally making up your mind.

With a four-function outfit, two functions are operated by each stick which can be moved in both vertical and horizontal directions at the same time. One then has to decide whether the primary functions, those that affect the directional control or speed, are to be on one stick or separated. The general consensus among boaters appears to favour the latter arrangement, in line with two-function outfits, with the auxiliary functions distributed to choice.

On most transmitters, sticks can be arranged self-centring, loaded by a spring, or progressive. Self-centring is

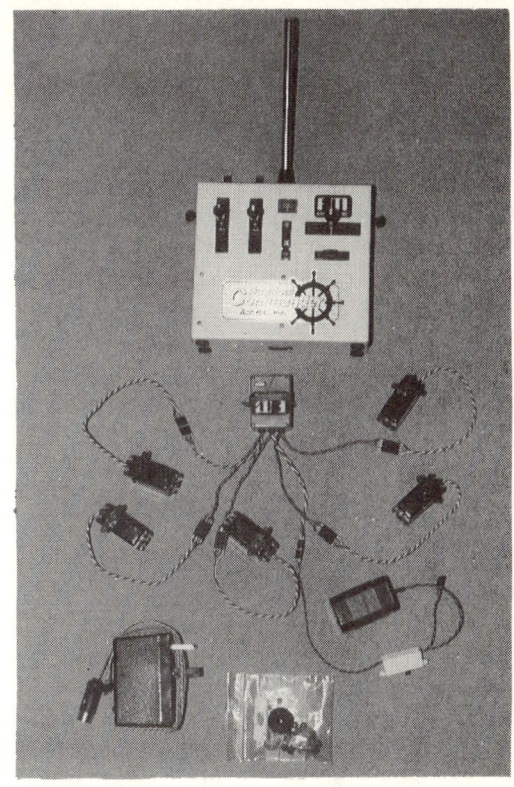

Tailor-made system by British manufacturer, specifically for a display model, featuring five servos.

self-explanatory, however progressive control is used on speed controls for instance, and the stick moved is 'held' in its last position by a friction device. Exactly the same kind of servo is used for each type; it is the mechanical action of the stick which determines the type of control. The trim facility, which I mentioned briefly earlier, provides approximately 10% of the servo movement in the direction in which the lever is moved, independent of the main control lever. This gives the facility of slightly shifting the servo disc to give an exact straight line on rudder or minutely adjust the throttle response during model operation.

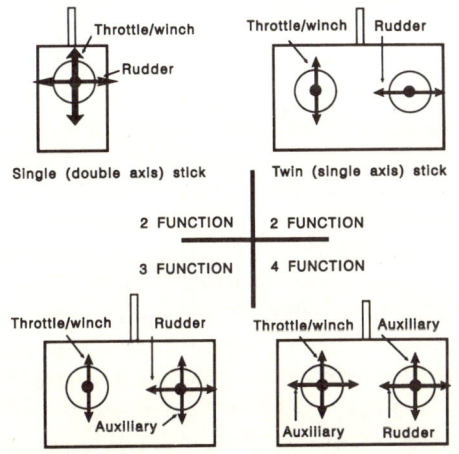

page 15

Chapter 2
What do we want to Control?

IN THIS chapter we take a look at what we are going to use the R/C system for, and discuss some of the major criteria affecting efficient operation of these items.

Rudders

The prime function of any R/C system is to control the directional motion of the model. With a model boat, in almost all circumstances, this is going to be via a rudder, although we must not forget the specialist Schottel and Voith Schneider swivelling propeller systems. However, even these can be considered as rudders in that the servo movement is still used to rotate the directional axis of the unit to change direction.

With scale ships and boats, using electric or steam power, it is unlikely that the loads generated on the servo disc by the force of water acting on the rudder blade will be so great that the servo will stall. So, in almost every case,

it is quite feasible to install a scale rudder as called for on the plans or supplied in the kit. There will be occasions, though, when one cannot obtain enough directional control and it may be necessary to increase the size of the rudder, or to move its location to a position where the water thrust from the propeller actually flows across the surface of the propeller. However, this is not a common problem.

With models propelled by internal combustion engines, or high power electric models, it may be necessary to install a balanced rudder. This is simply a matter of positioning the hinge line back from the leading edge so that part of the rudder is in front of this line and part behind. When operated, the impinging water stream on the front part helps to turn the rudder and once held in the turned position it continues to relieve the servo of the necessary forces that would otherwise be required to hold the position. A perfect balance is not required.

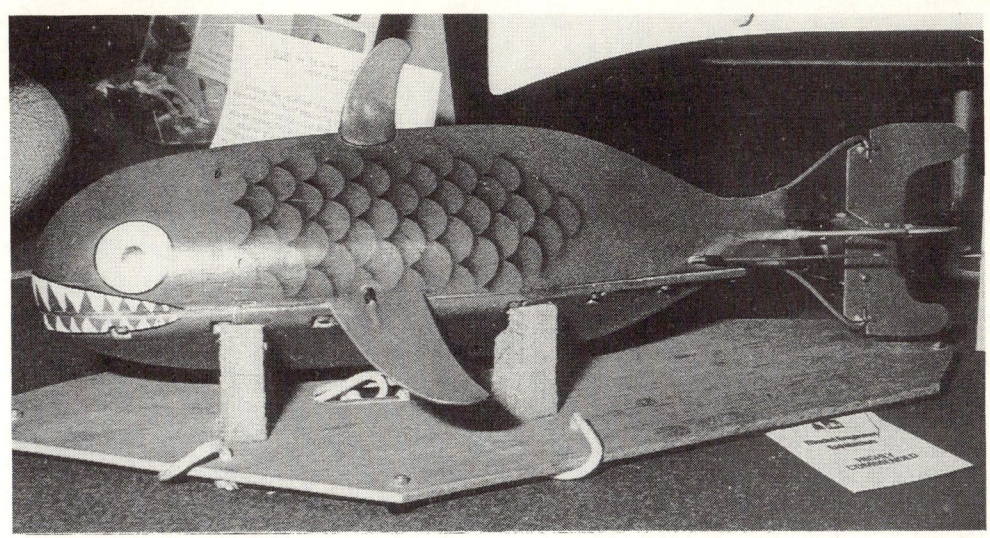

An unusual application for R/C. This submarine/fish? can even produce rolls and loops under water. *Photo: Ray Brigden.*

An R/C hydro is an exception in that its rudder is normally completely unbalanced, so in this case it will be necessary to purchase a high power servo and possibly link it to the rudder by a closed loop system (see Chapter Three). With model yachts, all designs drawn for R/C or kits will feature balanced rudders. However, if the design is for a vane boat, that is a non-radio boat, it is almost certain that a completely unbalanced rudder is shown, in which case a similar modification is called for as discussed with the internal combustion engined model. A balanced rudder will be very precise in its action, and 30 degrees or less of rudder movement in any one direction will be more than adequate and give the sharpest turns.

Engine Speed

In this instance, we need to control the speed of an internal combustion engine, a steam engine or an electric motor.

All internal combustion engines are available with R/C carburettors. In most cases it is only necessary to control the barrel or slide part of the carburettor, which controls the amount of air and fuel going into the engine, very similar to when you push the accelerator pedal on a car. However, unlike the car, there is no return spring and the servo must push and pull the carburettor arm to affect control. Some of the top of the range racing engines will also have a mixture control that can be adjusted while the model is in operation by means of a third servo. This facility can be particularly useful for long multi-boat races where engine temperature and fuel levels can have a marked effect on engine performance.

Steam engines can be very simple with no speed control facility at all, or they can have a steam control/reversing valve operated by a servo somewhat similar to the ic engine's carburettor system. Sophisticated steam plants may also have a gas control valve and again an extra third servo is required.

This oceangoing salvage ship is scratchbuilt from ASP plans and features working fire monitors. Other items such as the crane, anchors and winches, can all be made operational if desired.

Most model boats are controlled by electric power and there are mechanical and electrical controllers available. The simplest is switching a micro-switch using a servo, through resistance type speed controllers (see later) which also need a servo to operate them, to fully electronic speed controllers. These replace the servo and plug directly into the receiver. They give full proportional control and are very efficient. I will look at them in more detail in Chapter Five.

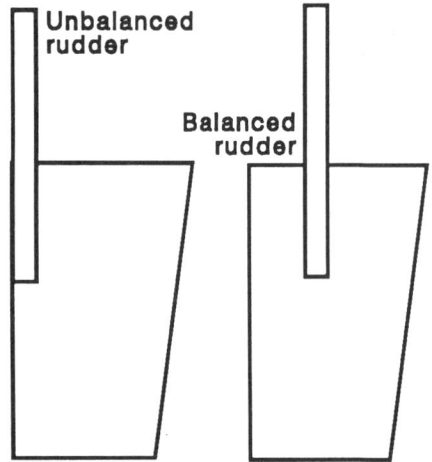

Unbalanced rudder

Balanced rudder

Sails

The driving force of a model yacht is its sails, and it is quite straightforward to set these in the optimum position if the yacht is to sail in one direction only, and the wind direction does not change! So, we need our R/C system to be able to alter the settings of the sails just as if we were sitting on board the yacht. Most model yachts use the Bermuda rig of two triangular sails, a jib and a main, and in almost all cases the job of the R/C system is to let out and pull in these sails to the best position for maximum drive from the wind and sails. The force required to adjust the sails varies according to their size and angle to the wind. Sheeting out offers no problems as the wind helps, but sheeting in when the sail is square to the wind may require up to 6 lb pull on a large suited 50" yacht in a brisk wind. Very small sails of around 1 sq. ft. can be adjusted by fixing a long lever arm onto a conventional servo. This is the system used by some of the smaller kit yachts approaching no more than 20" in length.

Another ingenious device is the una rig, a balanced cranked mast with fixed booms, but the system is still not completely proven as being equal to the conventional set-up, and is still limited to boats up to about 36" long. So a winch is a necessity for all but the exceptions mentioned above. The drum winch, as described in the chapter on the transmitter, is almost universal these days. The Americans and Europeans were rather fond of a lever winch for many years – basically a larger version of the modified servo system mentioned above for yachts under 20" – but that has lost favour over recent years. Scale sailing craft require special conditions as far as sheeting systems are concerned which really need to be

Finishing a course at the National R/C Scale Championships by bringing *HMS Avenger* into the dock. The judge on the pontoon checks to ensure a clean approach and docking.
Photo: Ray Brigden.

tailor-made to suit the particular craft in question; however in most cases a winch will still be required as the main function will be to operate the sails. I will look at some possible methods in Chapter Three.

Auxiliaries

Most R/C systems are used only to control rudder and speed, and there is much potential for operating other services. Most of the organised events in the UK are aimed at steering the model around a course, whereas many Continental regattas have events for demonstration models, both individual and in groups. These allow vessels to sound horns, operate water pumps, drop anchors, lower lifeboats, put out fires, turn gun turrets and fire guns, cast and recover fishing nets, etc.

Such events are at last starting to take

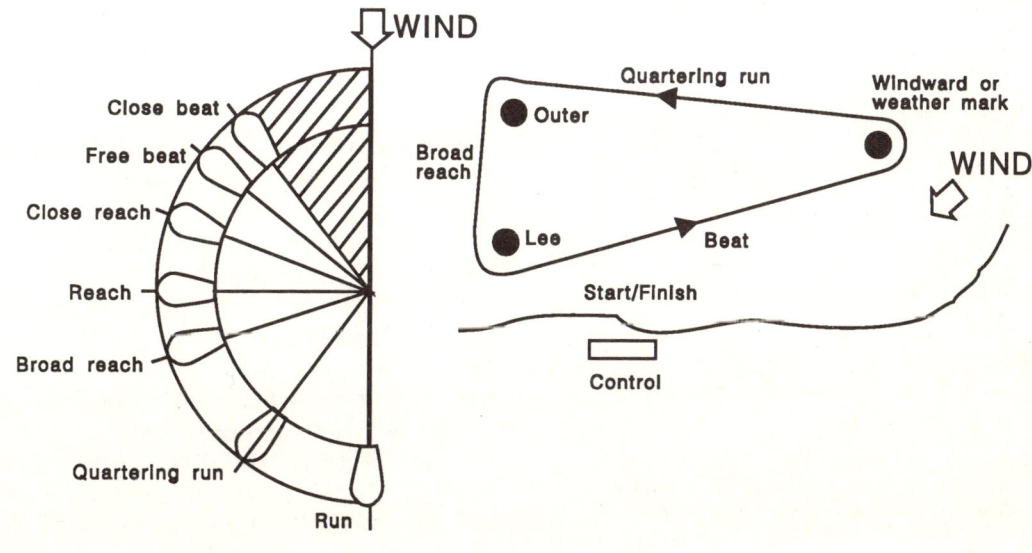

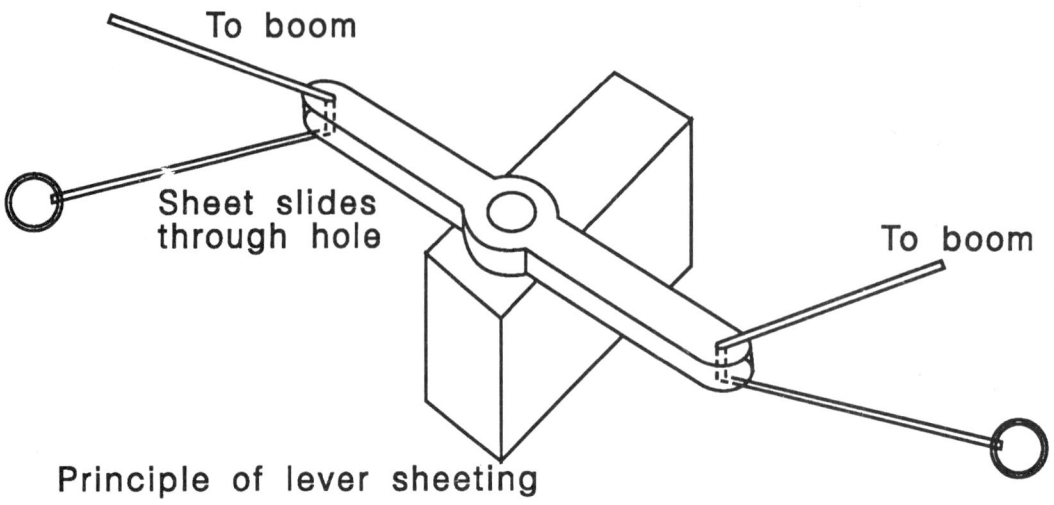

To boom

To boom

Sheet slides
through hole

Principle of lever sheeting

At World Championships, there are competitions for displays using many models and modellers. This French team is about to reconstruct the Spanish Armada battle with cannons blazing, ships burning and sinking!

place in the UK but, even if there is not one near to you, much fun can be gained at club and private levels with such models, and they are always very popular at public shows. Many of the devices mentioned above can be built with a little ingenuity and little expense, but all will require some method of control.

Full function R/C equipment designed primarily for R/C aircraft will offer six functions and require six servos, leaving four for auxiliaries once the rudder and speed controls are taken care of. It is not very often, however, that all the special functions will be in operation at one and the same time, and therefore one or two servos could be used to operate some form of sequential switcher.

A device similar to that shown in the figure can operate five switched services, three controlled by movement of the transmitter stick and hence servo one way with the other two in the opposite stick direction. A typical set up is: Radar on, Warning Lights on, Siren on in one direction of the servo, with Position Fire Monitor and Pump Water in the other. A progressive type stick

Another display at a World Championships. A Dutch team put out a fire on an oil rig and tow it to safety.

would obviously be the best choice to hold any one position as required.

There are a number of Continental R/C equipment manufacturers who

The internals of this German warship show the rotating cannon shell launcher used in displays. Five servos can also be seen, the rearmost driving twin rudders.

produce gear particularly for the boat modeller who specialises in display work, and between 12 and 32 extra services can be switched through a special receiver and control box. A number of domestic suppliers manufacture a 'black box' which plugs directly into the receiver in place of the servo and which can give up to six extra services from one function.

Devices such as sirens, monitors, etc., need to be operated from the R/C equipment. A model can be enhanced in its display characteristics by fitting one or more of the electronic noise generators now commercially available, or by building your own from one of the circuits published in *Radio Control Boat Modeller* magazine in recent years. Various noises are available, ranging from ships' diesels to a tug's steam

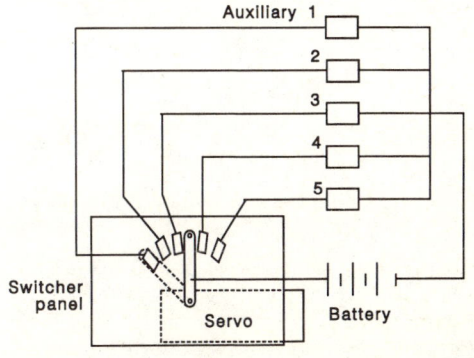

Wiper arm mounted on servo output spindle

A siren which can be activated by a switching system as an auxiliary component.

You are never too young to start boat modelling. These two, brother and sister, are taking part in the Junior section of the National R/C Scale Boat Championships. *Photo: Ray Brigden.*

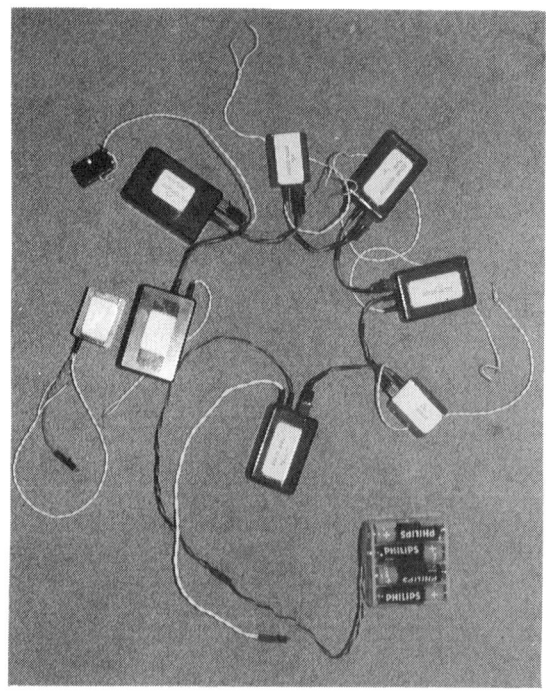

A selection of electronic devices: flashers, hooters, noise simulators, etc.

engine. They are wired into the drive motor supply leads and start operating as power is fed to the motor. If an electronic speed controller is used, some of these devices will pick up the changing pulses from the speed controller and use them to speed up or slow down the simulated engine noise in synchronisation with the speed of the motor and hence model.

When a steam powered model is combined with R/C, it is normal practice, of course, to control the rudder and engine speed. Steam engines always used to be controlled by a simple screwed needle valve but obviously this is not an easy device to operate by radio control, so either a taper plug cock type valve can be used, or a rotating disc type regulator. These are now available commercially: look in the advertising pages of the model magazines for specialist suppliers. Not all steam engines can be reversed and, if the model is to be steam powered under R/C, it is recommended that a twin cylinder double acting engine be used.

Recently some modellers have been experimenting with automatic boiler feed water suppliers and remote control of the firing system, particularly where gas burners are in use, as it is relatively straightforward to control gas flows with regulating valves operated by a servo. So, if you are thinking of steam power, it might be worthwhile considering purchasing R/C equipment with at least four functions.

Chapter 3
Where and How to
Position R/C Equipment

Planning the Installation

DON'T SKIP THIS BIT! In capitals to grab your attention because we rather fear that the above sub-heading may encourage some readers to skip this section; after all planning is boring! Boring it may be, but a few minutes spent here may save hours of frustration during the R/C installation process, so please bear with this bit. You will benefit, I promise you.

Don't jump in feet first in a rush to get the boat on the water – you will only spend longer on perpetual repair work when your friends are all enjoying themselves, and you are wondering why you are always so unlucky with your model. Luck has very little to do with it. Also, ignore the club know-all who informs you that 'waterproof' servos can be stuck straight down on the hull bottom with servo tape and all will be well. It won't be! 'Waterproof' servos are in general not waterproof – only water-resistant. There is a significant difference. They will resist the occa-sional splashes, etc., but they will not run for any length of time in a sub-merged environment. However well a model is constructed, water will find its ways inside through rudder tubes, pro-peller shafts, split water cooling pipes, etc., and what is the lowest part of the inside of a boat? – yes, the hull bottom, not the ideal place to stick servos.

Radio is so compact now that it can be fitted into most model boats, including many plastic kits. However, beginners are advised to build something rea-sonably large to start with, and a suggested rule of thumb is that, if you multiply the beam in inches times the length and obtain a figure greater than 120, you should have little difficulty.

In most models of this size factor and over, it should be possible to install all the radio gear, ie. receiver, batteries and servos, at least, in a waterproof compart-ment, and ideally in a waterproof con-tainer. Dampness is the arch-enemy of R/C equipment. An obvious statement, perhaps, but the number of model boaters who will allow their radio gear

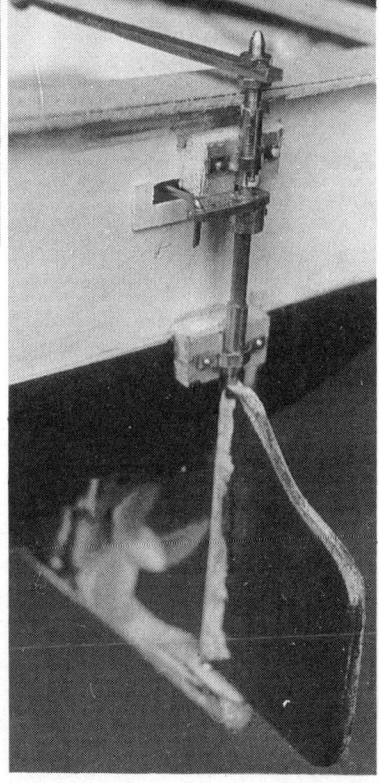

The Billing *African Queen* kit was never designed for R/C, so it is quite a challenge. There is a 'space' under the foredeck, but the cut-out in the main deck frame is the only access once deck is sealed in position, so the pencell nicads are charged *in situ* through a jack-plug built into the receiver switch. This is where a BEC system would be useful, (see Chapter Six). Timber blocks were needed to bring the rudder post away from the transom, to facilitate swing when the rudder servo linkage is added.
Photos: Ray Brigden.

literally to float in water is beyond belief. Suggest that they operate their portable TV or cassette player in a bucket of water and you get a very odd look, but there is no difference in the principle. A very popular choice for a container to take all boat radio gear is one of the large variety of lunchbox/food containers obtainable from High Street stores. These usually have a flush fitting lid and can be easily sealed with good quality adhesive tape. Freezer tape is ideal as it works well in damp and cold conditions. Alternatively you can purchase purpose-made boxes from your local model shop, available in a variety of shapes and sizes and usually supplied with switch, charging sockets, aerial socket, mounting brackets, etc. The only disadvantage in mounting the whole 'works' in one container is that, whereas the receiver and batteries can be surrounded by foam for anti-vibration and protection against impact, the servos need to be firmly fixed to the box to avoid sloppy control systems. The box must be firmly fixed to the model, of course. Also, make sure that effective linkages can be arranged to the rudder, throttle, etc.

Some kits, particularly fast electric-powered sports models, often include a plastic tray with holes and mountings suitable for the receiver, batteries and servos. Unfortunately, these are often only suitable for the make of R/C gear that the manufacturer of the boat wants you to use for commercial reasons. However, with most R/C systems becoming more and more similar in terms of size of components, it is not usually too difficult to modify the trays to allow other manufacturer's R/C systems to fit.

One problem with small equipment is that one is encouraged to build smaller models, and in many cases it is impossible to group the equipment together

The Wetbike from Robbe is an unusual model and operates well under R/C. There isn't much space inside the hull. From left to right: 7.2 volt, 1.2 ampere hour nicad battery pack, R/C car type high specification speed controller and steering servo can be seen. In models like this, the R/C gear has to survive in the prevalent conditions; no chance of nice waterproofed boxes.

because of space limitations, and the servos have to be mounted separately. In this case try to provide a watertight compartment and mount them as high as possible, away from any bilge water, and clear of splashes that find their way up rudder posts. You can wrap the receiver and battery in a small polythene bag which will keep the worst away. Wrap it in foam for vibration protection and include a small pack of silica gel. The latter is in the form of crystals and can be purchased from a chemist and put into small linen bags which should then be sewn up. The crystals have the property of attracting water and moisture and are particularly effective against condensation problems that can occur with sealed compartments due to temperature and humidity changes. It is necessary to dry out the crystals from time to time by placing them over a heat source such as a radiator.

The disadvantage with separately mounted servos is the extra time and fiddling required when changing the equipment to another model, unless of course you can afford separate servos for each model and simply change over the receiver and battery box.

Keeping Dry

As stated earlier, water ingress will certainly cause loss of control, which consequently could result in more physical damage and, while the receiver will probably escape from fresh water contamination, it will definitely not escape from the effects of sea water. Once water or even moisture has found its way into servos, it is impossible to remove by forced air drying but only by taking the unit apart. Furthermore, the very small motors used today in servos cannot be successfully dismantled by the modeller as they need specialist equipment. It is essential, therefore, that precautions are taken to keep at bay the substance which keeps our hobby afloat.

Assuming you have opted for the water-resistant box approach, it is necessary to fix firmly the servos to the box. For scale models, one can use self-adhesive double-sided servo mounting pads, but power models will require the servos to be fixed to wooden bearers which are themselves screwed to the box sides or base. The switch and charging socket can be positioned near to the top of the box, and a large blind grommet mounted in the lid of the box

immediately over the switch and be completely watertight. A similar system can be employed for access to the receiver crystal. The most awkward part of the installation will be the sealing of the various holes required for aerial lead, and operating pushrods. The aerial wire can either be routed through a rubber grommet or attached to a socket mounted in the side of the box with a matching plug to the wire leading away from the box.

Pushrods operated by linear action servos can be passed through a close fitting brass tube and smeared with silicone grease, but these type of servos have almost disappeared from R/C equipment these days and the system will not work with rotary output servos. There are a number of ways around this problem, the most preferred being rubber bellows, grommets or balloon necks. The grommets are commercially available. With snakes (see Chapter Four), the outer tube is simply epoxied or fixed with cyanoacrylate adhesive to the box side and led away through a suitable sealed hole (epoxy again), but the clearance required at the cable ends can make the box requirement too large. The box lid can be sealed with a smear of silicone grease and freezer tape, as mentioned previously.

As it is often necessary to strengthen a plastic lunchbox, especially if servos are to be included, many modellers opt

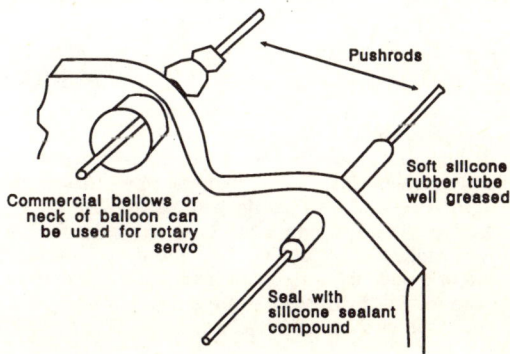

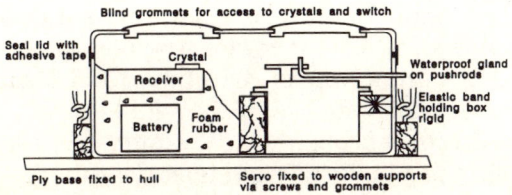

A system seen in the mid 1970s. The i.c. engine drives two screws through a gearbox. There is a servo to select the gears, just out of picture at the right, a second for throttle, a third amidships working a clutch, and a fourth at the stern turning twin rudders. The receiver is the forepeak and the batteries just aft of amidships. It would have been very difficult to fit a waterproofed box system in such a model.

to construct the entire box from ply, reinforced at the corners and top with small wooden bearers. A Perspex lid can be fitted with small screws and sealed with a smear of silicone grease. This form of construction enables the user to see that all is well inside (most plastic lunchboxes are opaque), and can of course be tailored to the individual model. If you have only fitted the receiver and battery box in the box, it will be sufficient to hold the box *in situ* with elastic bands secured to suitable hooks against a foam pad. However, if the servos are included, the box must be rigidly fixed and, if the equipment is to be used in other models, then it must be possible to accurately relocate the box when moving it from model to model. One method is to fix wooden bearers onto the hull bottom alongside the box sides and secure with heavy duty rubber bands. In glass-reinforced plastic hulls it is possible to mould grp pads directly from the box. Once the final positioning has been decided, clean and score the area on the hull bottom where the four corners of the box will fall. Smear a little silicone grease on the outside corners of the bottom of the box, mix up enough grp resin filler to split into four parts and apply this to the hull bottom where the corners of the box are to sit. Carefully lower the box onto the pads, apply a little pressure to create the shape and allow to dry. On removal of the box, you should find four perfectly moulded pads which will ensure that the box always goes back into exactly the same position. Again, suitable positioned elastic bands will hold everything in place.

If you decide to use the alternative method which turns a part of the model into a watertight compartment, many of the methods described above for sealing pushrods etc., can be applied. This system is probably more suited to sports and particularly multi boats, although a number of scale modellers also use variations of this idea. The compartment can be constructed by making use of the structural bulkheads of the model and easily sealed with a coat of grp resin. A frame needs to be fixed around the lip of the compartment where a clear Perspex or acrylic top can be fitted to facilitate inspection without removal. A sliding hatch is favoured by some modellers or the quick-release, half-turn screws. This will suffice for most models which are not expected to turn turtle or operate in rough conditions; however, for yachts or multi-race boats, this is not positive enough and a bolt or screw down system can be considered.

After providing the framing from .375" to .5" square wood, draw file the top flat. Fabricate the hatch from .125" or equivalent Perspex/acrylic sheet, and drill clearance holes around the edge of the sheet at approximately 2" to 3" centres to accommodate .5" long by No. 8 self-tapping screws. Then use the cover as a template to drill 3/32" holes in the wood framing and carefully drive home the screws. When fitting the cover in normal use, smear a thin film of silicone grease over the coaming and, as the hatch is screwed down and the surfaces come together, a clear indica-

This unfortunate receiver spent a week immersed after sinking. There are a number of corrosive deposits, especially on the pins at right, and the crystal is almost corrosion welded into its socket. *Photo: Mike Kemp.*

tion of a good seal is apparent. An alternative or an adjunct to grease is a thin rubber strip. This can be attached to the wood frame with a contact adhesive, or can be purchased from some model shops with adhesive on one side.

Fast access to the radio equipment is restricted with any system which includes some form of physical screw fixing, as it does take two or three minutes to gain entry, but this disadvantage is more than compensated for by the guarantee of absolute dryness. A further refinement with this system, especially suitable for submersible craft, is to fit a Schrader car type tyre valve in the hatch and apply a few pounds of air with a bicycle hand pump before sailing. The very slight positive air pressure will tend to push any water out. If the worst does happen and everything gets soaked, the first thing to do is to disconnect the batteries. It is the electrolytic effect of electricity and water combined that does the worst damage. Most of the solid state components used in the R/C gear will not be affected by a short dunking in fresh water, but salt water is a different ball game. The best action in the latter case is to take the gear to the nearest source of fresh water and

A typical sports boat installation. It is unlikely to turn turtle like a multi-race model, but the equipment needs protection from splashes etc., so the R/C box system is ideal. The box is positioned on pads moulded into the hull bottom as described in the text. Direct linkage to throttle passes over the top of the fuel tank.

attempt to wash out all traces of salt water. Then, and only then, should you dry out the equipment with the car heater or anything that features a moving stream of warm dry air. Electrical component or motor cleaners can be sprayed over the components to remove the final dregs of moisture, but don't use WD40 or similar preparations as these contain a waxy lubricant which attracts dust like the plague!

Scale Model Installations

Most scale model boat enthusiasts will have more than one scale model, hence the radio gear will need to be installed in a manner which allows for relatively quick removal and re-installation and yet, when in place, is rigidly positioned to facilitate precise control movement. The 'lunchbox' system is therefore very suitable.

For fixing the servos to the box or some other suitable surface raised clear of the hull bottom, double-sided adhesive servo tape is ideal. This can be purchased from model shops or radio accessory outfits. Some stationers sell self-adhesive strip and tabs designed for general office use, but this is not really sticky or strong enough. It will do in an emergency, though. The best of all is from the Japanese model car manufacturers – a thin flexible black rubber with fantastic adhesive and which, with care, can even be re-used a couple of times. The protective film should be removed from one side of the tape and the tape first applied to the servo. Then offer up to the proposed installation position and, when fully satisfied, clean the surface area, which must be smooth and dry, remove the second piece of protective film, and finally apply the servo with firm but gentle pressure. If the workroom is very cold, the adhesive

may lose a little of its stickiness, so apply a little heat from a fan heater or hair dryer. If you have stuck the servo in the wrong place, and on removal the strip tears, leaving half stuck on the servo and half on the model surface, this can easily be removed by applying a little enamel thinners or White Spirit with a paper towel or rag. Finally, it pays to inspect the strength of the bonds occasionally. Servo tape does not last for ever, especially in hot weather when it can simply peel away from the mounting surface of the servo.

For real security, wooden bearers can be fitted to the bottom of the box using woodscrews driven through from the underneath, or wooden rails can be fixed along the sides of the box; 6 by 6 mm strip will suffice. Don't forget to use the rubber grommets and eyelets usually supplied with your R/C gear when purchased for fixing down the servos. These allow a little flexibility to absorb shocks and vibration. If the lunchbox needs strengthening, a piece of ply the shape of the box bottom can be stuck in with contact adhesive.

The receiver can be fixed with servo tape direct to the box sides to a suitable tray. Foam wrapping is not really needed in an electric or steam powered scale model as there should be no vibration to worry about. The receiver battery pack can be fixed with servo tape, or wrapped in foam and allowed to sit in a suitable position in the box.

Steam powered models provide the worst possible conditions for R/C systems, as they are not only damp, but hot as well. It is almost mandatory for a separate sealed compartment to be provided, and the servos should be of the waterproofed type or sealed with silicone grease or contact adhesive. To effect this, carefully remove the fixing screws which hold the servo's plastic case together, and smear silicone grease

This Canadian tug includes what must be one of the most sophisticated R/C systems ever seen in a boat model. Everything was home-made, including the transmitter. Almost everything on the model that could move and be operated by R/C, does! *Photos: Ray Brigden*

or contact adhesive along all jointing surfaces. Don't forget the hole where the connecting lead emerges. Reassemble by gently tightening the screws. This method is quite effective. The contact adhesive is easily removed in the future by peeling away once the screws are loosened. A smear of grease around the servo output arm is also a good idea.

The enclosed compartment system can be taken a stage further for low freeboard models. Many small-scale models are asked to operate in water conditions that consistently mean decks are awash, and of course submarines are designed to go under the water, so instead of an R/C compartment, the whole of the engine compartment and radio area is constructed as a complete watertight container. This can be achieved using the same method of forming a relatively substantial lip around the whole of the compartmentalised area and screwing down a transparent hatch. The hatch needs to be a bit thicker than specified for just an R/C compartment, at least 5 mm thick. The Schrader tyre valve positive air pressure system described earlier is also of great value in these types of models.

Steam powered models are not only wet, they are hot and humid. All the R/C equipment is located, not very neatly, in the forepeak, but at least it's dry.

Racing and Internal Combustion Powered Model Installations

There are two major problems – the boats often end up inverted and there is

Typical racing i.c. model installation with completely sealed aft R/C compartment with clear plastic hatch securely held down with ten allen headed screws.

R/C hydroplanes are notoriously wet, so a sealed, bolted down compartment is the only answer for effective and dry R/C.

always engine vibration present – so it is ultra important that the R/C gear is situated in as protected an environment as possible. With sports models, the lunchbox arrangement can be used with the box mounted forward of the engine or in a compartment aft, such as the deck well in a cabin cruiser type model. Protection of the receiver and batteries by foam wrapping is essential. One useful source of protection is obtainable from plumbers' merchants. It is called Armaflex, an elastomeric nitrile rubber foam pipe lagging. This is a strong, dense foam and, as it comes in tube form, the battery pack can be slipped inside and the ends sealed with scrap. Obtained through the plumbing trade, Armaflex comes in two metre lengths which is far more than you will require for your immediate needs. If sharing the stuff around the rest of the club does not appeal, then Armaflex is available from some model shops in shorter lengths.

When positioning the pack and sliding on the foam, take great care not to strain the leadout wires. A broken wire would have disastrous results and a useful precaution is to double back the wire and tape it to the pack.

For multi-race boats, it is almost certain that the R/C installation will have to be in a watertight compartment at the extreme rear of the model. Races are relatively long and to carry enough fuel, which must be positioned as near to the centre of gravity of the model as possible to avoid altering the model's trim as the tank empties, the R/C gear is automatically despatched to the only remaining position in the model. One advantage is that the control links to the rudder will be short, but then of course the throttle linkage is going to be difficult.

The watertight compartment method already described can be used, or a commercial system can be purchased. The specialist racing boat model suppliers can provide radio boxes that are moulded into the model's hull and sealed with special rubber strips and quick release screws. The rudder shafts are double sealed to reduce water ingress to an absolute minimum, also.

Before leaving racing models, there is one other category that causes special problems – fast electric models. As we said earlier, internal combustion engined racing boats have their radio installations influenced by the position of the fuel tank. Similarly, fast electric

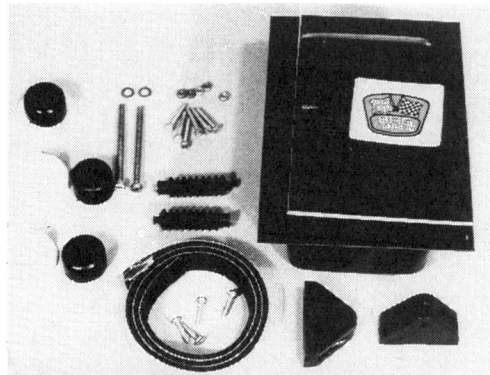

Fast electric models have no room for R/C boxes or anything of an extraneous matter as low weight is very important. The top is simply a piece of acetate film held down with self-adhesive tape.

A typical commercial radio equipment box in kit form and assembled. The plastic plugs enable access to on/off switch and to receiver crystal. The two jack-plug sockets are for charging the receiver nicads. Rubber bellows allow movement of servo linkages.

models have theirs dictated by the drive battery location, which never usually leaves an area suitable for a separate radio box installation. The aim with all electric boats is to keep the weight of the model to an absolute minimum, demanding that the receiver and servos will have to operate in undesirable locations. Indeed, almost every fast electric model you look into breaks all the previous rules and principles I have so far expounded in this book! But this is the price one has to pay for a competitive performance with a fast electric model.

Some kit manufacturers supply a moulded plastic tray to accept the servos, but again these are often quite heavy. One alternative is a lightweight aluminium tray similar to that shown in the figure. This can also be used for internal combustion engined powered boats if desired.

The general fate of the receiver and batteries is to wrap them in foam and place in a polythene bag. Regular maintenance and removal from the model after every outing is essential.

Despite the fact that an internal combustion engine running at 20,000 rpm is generating some 300 miniature explosions every minute, and transmitting this vibration throughout the entire model, most modern R/C systems are well able to withstand this

An electric hydroplane is again, a rather wet model so the whole rear compartment is sealed, this time with adhesive tape. *Photo: Glynn Guest.*

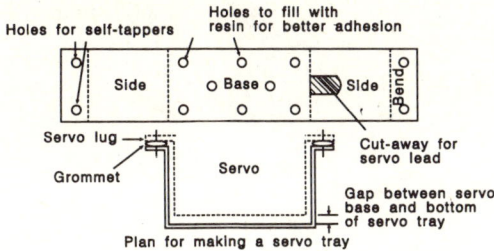

Holes for self-tappers
Holes to fill with resin for better adhesion
Side
Base
Side
Base
Servo lug
Grommet
Servo
Cut-away for servo lead
Gap between servo base and bottom of servo tray
Plan for making a servo tray

kind of abuse. But please wrap the receiver and battery pack in foam, and use the servo's mounting washers. An often overlooked result of this vibration is its effect on soldered joints which can simply break down and crumble under prolonged onslaught.

Sailing Model Installations

Model yacht decks probably spend more time under water, or at least are almost constantly awash, than any other model boat except for a submarine, so once again the prime requirement is to keep things dry. There are also long runs of cords called 'sheets' running around the model and up through holes in the decks to operate the sails. Finally, where the fast electric requires as little weight as possible for best performance, the yacht demands that all weight be kept as low as possible so the model sits as upright as possible (called 'stiffness') and obtains the maximum benefit from the wind.

So, life is a compromise again between best performance and mounting the R/C gear as high and dry as possible. If you want to be really competitive and are prepared to accept the risks, then sit your radio in a watertight box as low as you can; some modellers now even set their nickel cadmium batteries in resin in the actual bulb keel of the yacht! The best place is just aft of the mast, near to

This shot of an R/C Marblehead really shows how wet yachts are with the deck almost awash.
Photo: Mike Kemp.

A useful building accessory is this winch/servo cradle which suits the Whirlwind winch, a very well known winch in the world of model yachting. *Photo: Mike Kemp.*

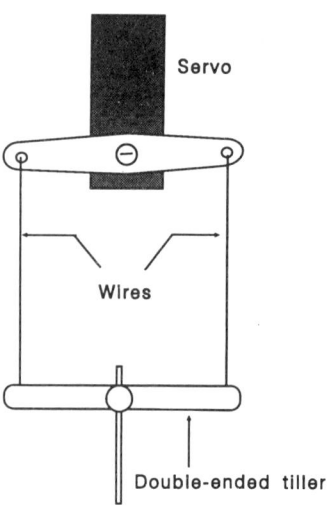

the centre of gravity, and immediately under an access hatch, made as water-tight as possible. Flush fitting hatches are pretty but usually much more difficult to seal than the raised type. For the seals to be fully effective they need to be under slight compression when the hatch is closed. The most positive method is to use screw fixings. An alternative approach is to simply cover the hole with polythene sheet and seal the edges with a good quality adhesive tape such as freezer tape. Not the most elegant or engineered of systems, but it seems to work, although a clash of boats can easily tear a hole in the polythene and then it's wave goodbye time! The separate, sealed box is still probably the best approach for most, and many yacht kit manufacturers now include a suitable box or pot – as they are often rounded – with their kits.

The pot normally houses receiver, batteries and on/off switch, and is mounted through a plate fixed across the beam of the yacht, usually the deck. The rudder servo and sail winch are then installed alongside or adjacent. The plate can simply be held in place by adhesive plastic tape. In a ply deck it can be screwed and glued in.

A disadvantage with the pot system and 'loose' servo/winch is the difficulty in swapping between boats, so the box in which everything can be fitted just wins on points.

Frequent access to crystal changing is often necessary when racing. With the pot it is simply a matter of unscrewing the lid to gain access and with the box the rubber plug system mentioned earlier can be used. Or, a crystal switcher can be included. The latter is a small plate carrying six crystal sockets and crystals, the sockets being wired to a multi-position selector switch. The system seems to work for many, but I do not recommend it as there can be problems with the switch contacts and with some receivers the extra lengths of wire involved give interference problems.

The rudder will be controlled by a servo mounted in the box or on separate rails, and controlled by a long link, or often a 'closed loop' system is used. The latter uses a double-sided tiller connected on each side to the respective sides of the servo output disc, using thin wire for operating rods. The advantage with this system is that rudder control is more positive and precise since the rudder is always pulled to one side or the other instead of, with a single rod, pulled one way and pushed the other. The rudder tube may end just below deck level, which often requires another hatch for access, or can be brought up through the deck. While this eases the method of firmly supporting the rudder and removes the need for a hatch, the disadvantage is another hole through the deck for the rudder linkage or servo output arm.

For racing models, a spade rudder is virtually universal. This is a fully-moving blade with no fixed skeg, usually pivoted 25–30% of its area back from the leading edge to provide dynamic balanc-ing which reduces the load on the servo. The blade is normally very narrow and deep, to retain effectiveness at large angles of heel and to reduce induced drag. Drag reduction may appear to be infinitesimal, but if it makes a difference of a few inches in a race, it may mean the difference between winning or losing.

The positioning of the winch very much depends on what type of sheeting system you intend to use so refer to the next chapter which discusses the various methods. However, whether located amidships or at the stern, it is important that the winch is very firmly located as the tension on the sheets can be quite substantial.

Chapter 4
Making a Good Connection

Electrical Connections

SWITCHES CAN be prime sources of trouble when they get damp and, even if looked after carefully, they do not last for ever. Springs break, contacts become dirty and corroded, and it's all hidden away until the day it doesn't work. So, first keep them dry, and secondly change them after a couple of year's use. If you can, site them near to the receiver crystal access hatch so that switching off/on and changing frequencies can both be carried out by removing only one access point. With models carrying a large amount of rigging and complicated or delicate superstructures, it can sometimes be difficult, or at the least time consuming, to gain access into the model just to switch on or off. The

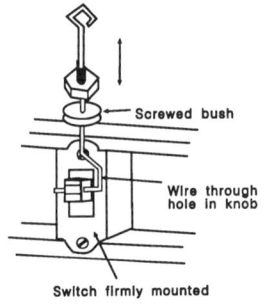

Screwed bush

Wire through hole in knob

Switch firmly mounted

switch can then be mounted remote from the receiver – if necessary the wires can be extended by soldering or a purchased extension lead. The switch can then be hidden under a deckhouse, hatch or some other disguised position. Don't forget regular inspections for corrosion.

An alternative approach is to operate the switch by a wire push rod which passes through a close fitting, grease-filled bush mounted on the side of the radio box or compartment. Switches can also be obtained which will operate by sliding a magnet over their surface.

Aerials

The basic principle when installing the aerial is that the total length of the wire attached to the receiver should not be lengthened or shortened during the installation. The first decision to make is do you require an outside aerial? An inside aerial should give at least 80 metres range which should be ample for all scale models. Make sure when routing the aerial wire away from the receiver box that it does not run parallel to any other wiring, and keep it away

Receiver and switch hidden under a removable deck, while servos are all below in this scale sailing model.

from the drive motor or motors and their associated wiring. Attaching to the underneath of the decks with servo tape is often a good method. As long as the aerial length is maintained, there is no reason why aerials cannot be made a part of the rigging of ships or a length of ship's railing.

Despite the fact that the R/C equipment will operate at up to 80 metres with the receiver aerial inside the model, for any type of boat powered by an internal combustion engine or a fast electric motor, it is essential that an exterior whip or telescopic aerial is fitted. Even if you operate alone, the

extra signal strength obtained will markedly reduce the possible loss of control which is the last thing one wants with a fast model turning a propeller at considerable revs which can cause physical damage to persons and property.

Whip or telescopic aerials can be purchased commercially or home-made. Telescopic aerials have almost disappeared now as they are prone to damage and relatively expensive. The whip aerial uses a piece of easily obtainable piano wire and is almost indestructible.

The figure shows one method of construction. It is no good just using a banana plug or jack plug to fit the aerial to the boat as this will eventually work loose, especially with engine vibration, and create electrical interference and bad contact causing loss of control. Once again, don't forget to maintain original aerial length. For example, if the receiver wire was 20", and you fit a 12" long whip aerial, then the length of wire from the aerial socket to the receiver must be 8". And, finally, don't forget to bend a loop on the top of the whip to prevent injury to eyes and person. Some modellers use a cork

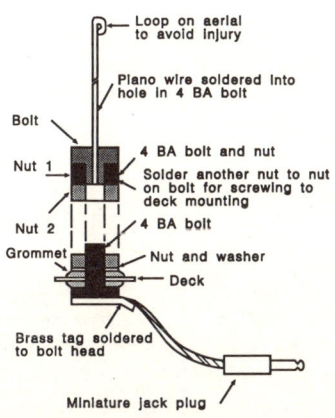

Loop on aerial to avoid injury

Piano wire soldered into hole in 4 BA bolt

Bolt

Nut 1

4 BA bolt and nut
Solder another nut to nut on bolt for screwing to deck mounting

Nut 2

4 BA bolt

Grommet

Nut and washer

Deck

Brass tag soldered to bolt head

Miniature jack plug

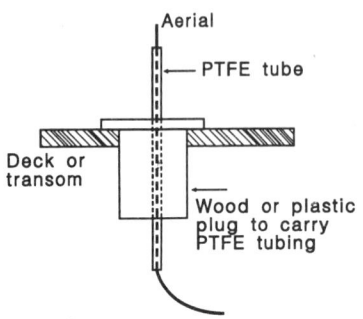

Aerial

PTFE tube

Deck or transom

Wood or plastic plug to carry PTFE tubing

pushed onto the aerial tip but this is not really adequate as it can easily be dislodged. The siting for the aerial should be as close to the receiver as possible and also as far away as possible from any potential source of interference or electrical noise, not always so easy, particularly with fast electrics, but aim for the best compromise.

For model yachts, again an underdeck installation is not recommended as almost all sailing will be in competition against other models, and often at some distance from the operator. The wire from the receiver can be led through a sealed outlet and run up the backstay or similar rigging wire and held with insulating tape. Don't fit a wire whip aerial and forget the swing of the

booms! It has been done! A useful tip from the R/C model car fraternity is to use a length of PTFE tubing with its inside diameter just larger than the aerial wire diameter. A wood or plastic plug can be drilled to accept the PFTE tube as a tight fit, and the plug inserted and fixed into a suitably sized hole in the deck. The aerial wire is simply fed up through the PTFE tube, turned back on the tube and secured with a turn of adhesive plastic tape.

Finally, before leaving aerials, transmitter aerials used in all MYA (Model Yachting Association) events must have a plastic golf ball fitted on their ends to prevent injury to other competitors during the 'walkabouts' that are now a feature of most R/C yacht races.

Physical Connections

After expending a not inconsiderable sum of money on purchasing your R/C gear and model, and no doubt a similar amount of time and energy in constructing the model, it is no doubt a quirk of human nature that the precise and efficient operation of the whole system may be spoilt by neglecting a part of the installation which will cost something

Puffer steering gear was in the form of a chain system from the steering wheel to the tiller, which has been copied in miniature form on this model.

40

less than 2% of the total expenditure. From inspection of many models experiencing radio gear failure or inaccurate control, it is apparent that the most common cause can be traced to bad installation of the mechanical connections or linkages between servos and operating surfaces.

Today's servos are marvellous examples of precision engineering and involve some of the most modern techniques to provide a strong, reliable, mechanism capable of giving accurate resolution of control signals to tolerances below 1%. It is an insult to this technology and a waste of money to use a bent piece of wire and mutilate the servo arms to achieve a solid, tight linkage that removes any possibility of achieving the wonderfully accurate con trol that is offered by modern proportional R/C systems.

There is one overriding factor with regard to the subject of servo linkages: *A servo should never be forced to overload or stall by tight linkages, rudder posts, throttle arms, etc. Everything should be precise yet free to move easily.* There are three basic methods adopted by the R/C fraternity: Pushrod, Tube or Closed Loop. The first two are the most popular and are normally used for rudder and

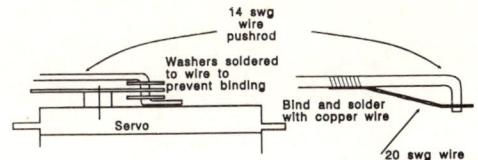

throttle; the closed loop system is not particularly easy to set up, but is a much more precise system where heavy loads or long fixed linkages are required, such as a hydroplane's or yacht's unbalanced rudder.

The best system in any mechanical set-up is usually the simplest and the pushrod certainly falls into this category. Pushrods for model boat use are not required to be as light as those used for model aircraft which use balsa and wire, but can be constructed from wire rod, easily obtainable. 16 swg (1.5 mm) is about the right size, obtainable from model shops, or some modellers use bicycle spokes. The model shop wires usually have one or both ends screwed to accept an adjustable clevis, a springy piece of forked metal or a plastic moulding which clips onto the servo arm or rudder/throttle linkage through suitably drilled holes, and which is threaded on the other end to screw onto the wire rod and give the facility to adjust the length of the linkage. This adjustment allows for final precise setting of the linkage in case of slight errors when positioning the servo.

Home-made pushrods can be produced by simply bending to the Z shape on their ends as shown in the figure. This can be achieved by careful use of thin, long-nosed pliers if such a tool is already in your tool box. If not, you would be well advised to purchase a neat tool which will easily form the bends for you and also provide a wire cutting facility. The washers shown are not usually needed when using the tool, but with pliers it is not easy to obtain a sharp radius on the bends and the

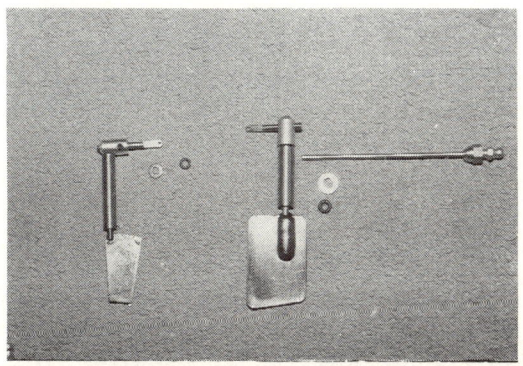

Left, an unbalanced rudder which needs considerable servo force to operate; right, a partially balanced rudder, much better for the servo and in most instances, better also for the model in terms of improved control.

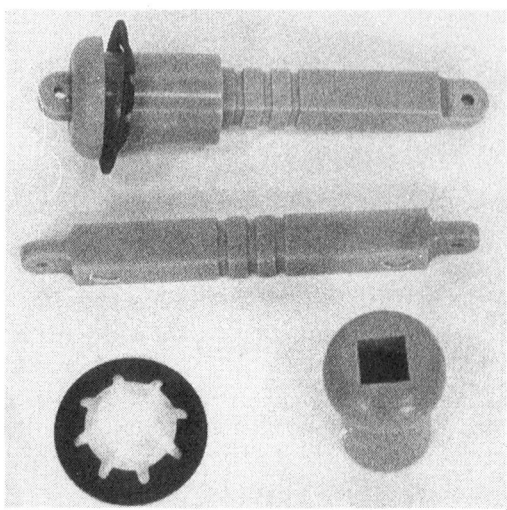

A commercial link for R/C box sides. The round plastic plug is fitted in the side of the box; the square slider can be greased in the three grooves for easy action and to prevent water entering the box.

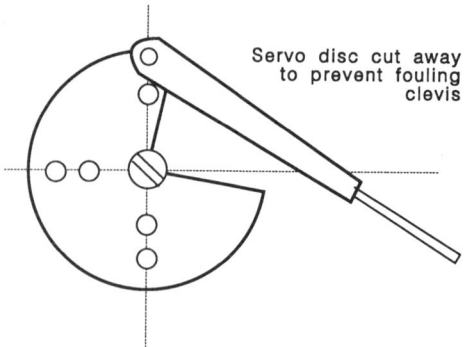

Servo disc cut away to prevent fouling clevis

washers will prevent binding on the output disc or arm in these circumstances.

An alternative to the Z shape is simply to bend the wire into the L shape shown. To prevent the linkage working free, it is necessary to remove the servo disc and to mount the L pin facing upwards. This method will only work on rotary discs where the servo top prevents drop out. A better solution which will work on all output arms, is to fabricate the keeper wire as shown, or purchase special plastic keepers which do the same job.

Commercial clevises and screwed ends can be purchased for fitting onto your own wire links, although an 8BA threading die will be required to thread 14 swg rod. Alternatively. there is an adaptor which can be soldered onto wire rod and a clevis is then screwed onto the exposed threaded end of the adaptor. There is an incredibly wide selection of commercial accessories in this area – it is practically an industry in

its own right – and a few minutes spent in your local model shop taking stock of what's available is time well spent.

An unfortunate problem with clevises as opposed to Z and L links is the possibility of the forks of the clevis jamming on the edge of the output disc. So, during the set-up and testing, operate the servo through maximum throw plus trim to ensure that this problem does not occur. It may be necessary to cut away part of the disc as shown.

All clevises which work on the fork principle will obviously jam the servo operation should the radio system become unstable – eg. in the case of bad interference – and this stalled condition can cause major damage to the servo amplifier components. This can be totally avoided by using the ball and socket system. The metal or plastic ball is screwed onto the output arm and held in place by a locking nut. The plastic socket is a push fit over the ball and, once in place, it is capable of being rotated through any horizontal and limited vertical angles with no binding or slop. These joints are still regarded by some as unreliable but that reputation, which was gained from their earlier days, is now completely discounted. Indeed the R/C model car world uses them almost universally and under much greater shock loads than will ever be experienced in any model boat, so perhaps a

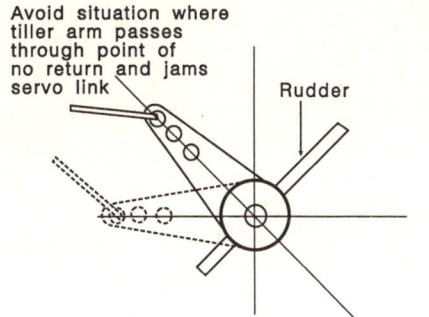

Avoid situation where tiller arm passes through point of no return and jams servo link

Rudder

close look at the R/C car counter of your model shop is in order!

Equal or Unequal Movement

Ensure that the angles between the rudder arm and the linkage and the linkage and the servo disc are at right angles, to ensure equal control surface movements with equal servo movements. This will also prevent the situation arising where the extreme control surface arm position, particularly rudder, together with any inherent play in the linkage, may allow the arm to flip over to the beyond-point-of-no-return position. A frequent cause of excess play, especially in lightweight glass reinforced plastic or styrene hulls, is the flexible nature of the hull, allowing movement at the top of the rudder post. This can be prevented by fixing a substantial wooden block across the bottom of the hull or by using a support connected to the transom or a bulkhead adjacent to the top of the tube.

During the pre-installation testing stage to determine linkage positions and lengths, you should have checked the servo movements to make sure that they operated in the correct sense or handing, ie. left on the rudder stick gives left on the rudder, and that the amount of movement given at the control surface would not be too large or small for the desired effect.

If the sense is incorrect you can change to the other side of the disc, although this can give unfavourable linkage geometry, or it may be more desirable to reverse the direction of the servo, either by operating the servo reversing switch if your system has this facility, or by purchasing an opposite-handed servo.

To obtain equal movement of control surface arm as compared to servo output arm, the radii of the disc and control surface must be identical. Extended arms can be purchased for servos, giving a greater movement at the control surface arm, or by also extending the control surface arm. If the same freedom of fit is involved as on the shorter arms, then the whole system will incorporate a relatively lower freedom factor and be more precise. Most rudders are at their maximum efficiency at 25 degrees either side of neutral. Going above this simply turns the rudder into a brake and puts extra load on the servo.

Occasions arise when unequal control surface movements are desirable, ie. a model which turns more one way than the other, or to obtain more movement at the throttle arm if the servo does not have enough initial throw, and the figure explains the theory behind differential linkages.

For throttle linkages, it is seldom possible to obtain a straight run and pushrods cannot normally be used. It is usually the fuel tank that prevents this, especially in multi boats where large

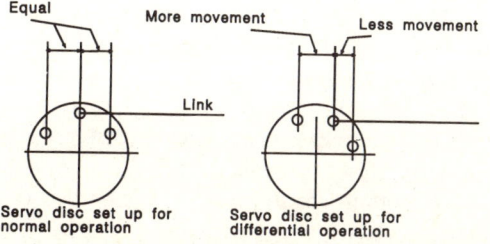

Equal   More movement   Less movement

Link

Servo disc set up for normal operation   Servo disc set up for differential operation

The snake linkage to the carburettor throttle can be seen, as can the whip aerial and on/off switch. This is a speed model, so is only expected to be run for very short periods, probably two or three minutes, so there is no risk of the switch becoming waterlogged.

capacities are required for long races. However, if using metal tanks, one dodge is to solder a brass or copper tube right through the centre of the tank to accept the pushrod. This is easier said than done, though, and fortunately the snake or tube solves the problem in a different way. These consist of a stranded wire or nylon rod running in a larger diameter nylon tube. The tube can be 'snaked' around obstacles, hence its name. More space at the servo end is required to allow sufficient sideways movement of the inner core of the snake, and it is important to fix firmly the outer tube to some part of the model structure at a number of points. Again a wide variety of clevises and adjusters can be used with snakes, and investigation at the local model shop is recommended.

The snake system is easy to use and

has proved popular among boaters, but it is this ease and versatility that causes modellers to demand too much from it and expect it to run around the model until it resembles a bunch of spaghetti. Every bend creates more drag and end float, and poorly supported and anchored tubes can lead to centring problems. So keep snakes as short and as straight as possible.

A straighter run to the engine can sometimes be obtained by running the snake along the side of the model and providing a bellcrank arrangement at the motor mount. This method also removes the linkages from possible conflict with the starting cord or belt. Remember, though, that it reverses the mode of operation. A range of holes in the throttle lever arm will give flexibility in initial setting up of the system so that full travel of the throttle arm matches full travel of the transmitter stick. It is important that these movements match. If, for example, the push-pull movement of the servo is greater than that permitted at the engine, then the servo will stall at one or both ends of its travel. This is very undesirable and will cause damage to the servo, either mechanically or electrically, and possibly even rapidly drain the receiver batteries to a point where control of the model is lost.

A slip link or spring loop can be built into the system to eliminate this problem, and the simplest type of link is a piece of silicone tube slipped over the pushrod. The spring loop is also fairly easy to make but requires a little soldering with fuse wire as binding.

With a little effort, neither of these devices should be required. What is important is that the idling speed is set up correctly, since in most cases the actual slow speed position is determined by the idling screw stop adjustment. If the extreme movements of the servo are matched to this, then full throttle posi-

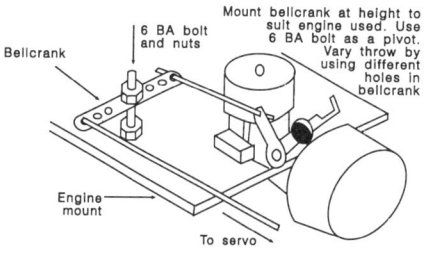

Bellcrank

6 BA bolt and nuts

Mount bellcrank at height to suit engine used. Use 6 BA bolt as a pivot. Vary throw by using different holes in bellcrank

Engine mount

To servo

Installation in an RM. The servo and winch tray will fit beneath the two holes forward of the round hole which is for the pot. The servo and winch are mounted at an angle to give the best direction to the linkages and sheets. *Photo: T Reece.*

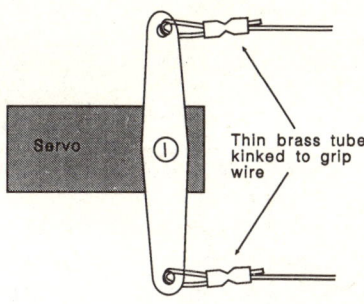

tion will leave a little tolerance, and in most cases it will be found that a slight discrepancy at the top end will have no effect on maximum speed of the engine.

It is a good idea to make use of the trim facility on the transmitter as follows. Back this off to the full throttle position and adjust the pushrod or snake so that when throttle closed is signalled by the transmitter the throttle moves to its normal idling position as established by the idling screw on the carburettor. The screw is then completely backed off, taking care not to go too far so that it drops out or can vibrate out. The transmitter will then give complete control with the trim in the forward (normal) position, but knock the trim back at tickover and the engine will stop, giving absolutely full control over the power plant.

In the closed loop system the servo pushes and pulls at the same time. This prevents the side and bending forces on a link and on the servo output shaft, and is particularly suitable for systems where power is called for. It can also be of benefit in certain scale models where rudder chains or cables travel through runners or pulleys along each side of the wheelhouse and/or bulwarks from the steering wheel to the rudder capstan.

The lines on the model can be terylene or nylon (fishing trace is ideal) and allowed to change direction over polished wire guides or pulleys or through rings. The wire can be secured after passing through the tiller arm or servo arm by sliding a short length of thick-walled, soft brass tube over the wire and crimping as shown in the figure. Purpose-made crimps can be obtained from model shops selling model aircraft accessories.

If you need to operate a twin rudder installation, this can be achieved by using a bellcrank fitted to one rudder, with its fore and aft arm linked to a fore and aft tiller on the other. The arm lengths of the bellcrank can also be altered to provide differential movement if required. Remember that the bellcrank will reverse the mode of operation.

To join wire rods without access to soldering equipment, use the metal centres of so-called 'chocolate blocks' or electrical wiring terminal blocks.

Piano wire that breaks on bending needs annealing. This can be accomplished by heating to red heat and allowing to cool slowly.

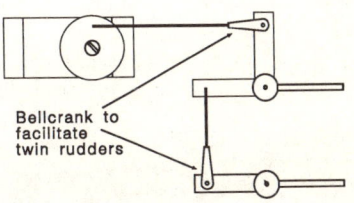

Metal to metal joints should be avoided since they can produce electrical interference with radio reception.

Yacht Sheeting Systems

As I mentioned earlier, the sail lever arm winch is almost non-existent now except in the smaller models, less than 20" overall length usually, and even in models of this size it is very easy to overload the servo mechanics and electronics. If you are using the system, try to make all turn points for the sheets as free as possible by running them through smooth rings. These can be made by cutting from plastic tubes and smoothing the edges with flourpaper or fine wet and dry paper.

For anything other than these small models, it is a complete waste of time trying to make a servo perform sail control. Any mechanical system can only give an output less than the original force output of the servo at a given speed so, even if you could gear the servo to give enough pull to operate sails, the speed would be so slow, and speed is important in any model which is to be used for racing, no more than 3 to 4 seconds from sails fully out to fully in and vice versa.

The drum winch is, therefore, almost universal. The normal amount of sheet movement obtainable from the drum is around 20" and of course this can be adjusted by using slightly larger or smaller drums. Some systems also

The immersed receiver seen earlier came from this pot which had only taken in a few drips of water during its week underwater. Enough to cause problems to the receiver, but the amount shows how well the system will work under normal operating conditions.

allow the total sheet travel to be adjusted by a trimmer on the winch, from say 15" to 20". The winch is a much more solid beast than a servo and usually has mounts to allow side or bottom fixing. Winches are also usually more water resistant than the servo as many are asked to perform in an above deck environment.

Most yachts operate with what is called a 'synchronous sheeting system', ie. the jib and main sail are controlled by the one winch drum or drums. The usual material for the sheet is sea fishing line or braided Dacron, a remarkably strong and flexible cord, yet with minimal stretching and low friction. The largest, heaviest 'A' Class boats will need 100 lb strain cord. The sheets will obviously need to pass through the deck at some point if the winch is located below deck, and this is a potential point of water

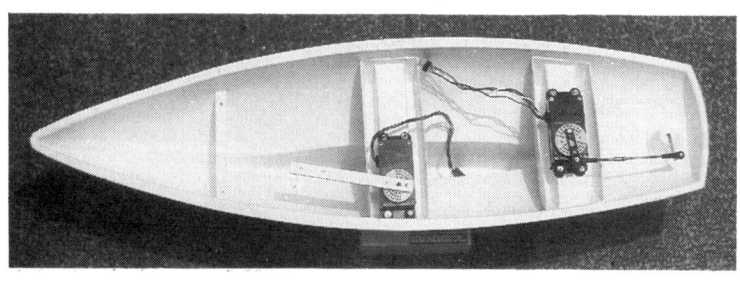

The 575 yacht is less than 20" long, and so a normal servo with a lever arm is just about strong enough to handle the sails in most conditions.

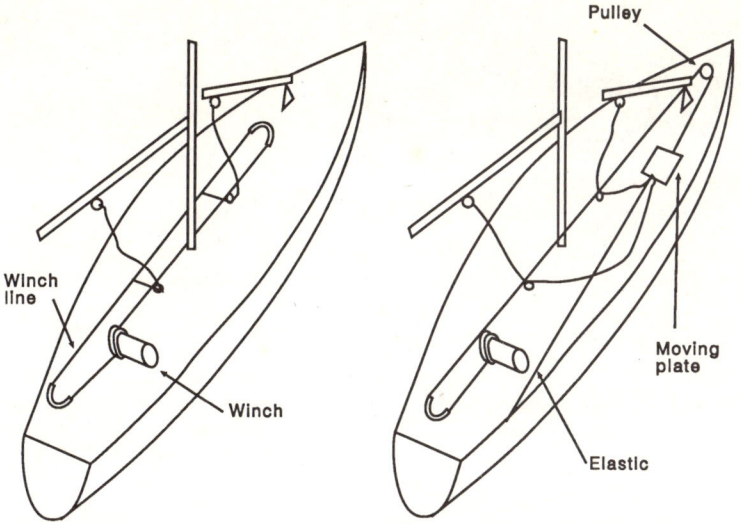

Pulley

Winch
line

Winch

Moving
plate

Elastic

Sheeting systems using double drum winch and continual loop,
and single drum winch with elastic as tensioner

ingress. While this cannot be entirely prevented, it can be markedly reduced by careful design and positioning of the leads. Again, low friction materials such as PTFE or nylon are best.

The leads can be angled away from the direction of flow should the boat ship water, which will restrict water intake. Alternatively, a tube can be brought some distance above the deck and the sheets led away through wire tripods above the tubes. If you opt for the system whereby the winch is mounted just below the deck with the output

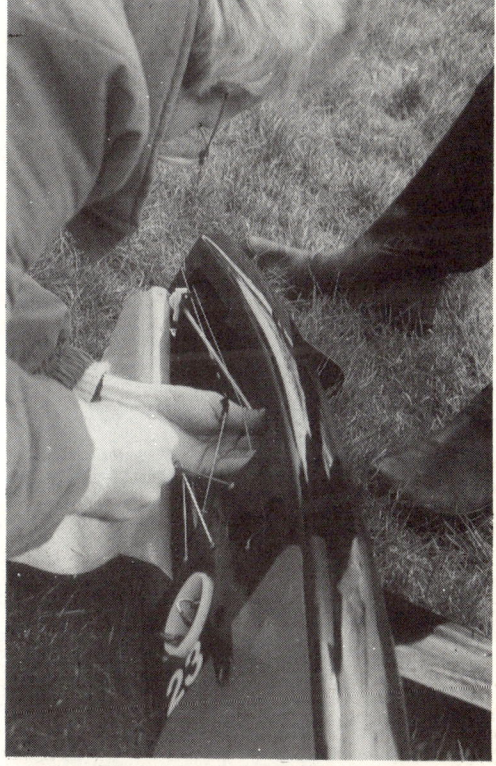

This grp RM yacht required major surgery to its rudder during a race meeting. Access was easy because of the completely removable sheet, secured with adhesive tape. Only problem with such systems is that they are prone to damage. *Photo: Mike Kemp.*

A very clean deck arrangement on this one metre boat. The deck is made from four pieces of ply. Uses pot and through deck winch system. *Photo: Mike Kemp.*

Access into this yacht is via a recessed hatch sealed with tape. Note the high sheet outlet. *Photo: T Reece.*

Rudder servo and sailwinch mounted alongside one another on a tray underneath the deck. Sheet emerges through outlet aligned aft to reduce water ingress. *Photo: T Reece.*

spindle protruding through a suitable hole, the latter can be sealed by a greased rubber O ring.

The simplest method of arranging the sheets is to take both directly from the drum, or from each drum if a two-drum winch. Sheet total travel will then be equal to the maximum travel of the winch. Sometimes the two drums will be of different diameters and the usual approach here is to attach the main sheet to the larger drum and the jib to the smaller, allowing the main sheet to be attached further aft on the main boom and giving a better mechanical advantage to the system. The snag with this arrangement is that the wind pressure on the sails is the only force keeping the sheets taut. In calm conditions or a sudden lull, the sheets can go slack and unwind from the drum. Artificial tension can be imparted on the system from a length of rubber as shown. The disadvantage, of course, is that the winch has more work to do.

A much better arrangement, now used by almost all model yachtsmen, is for the winch drum to drive an endless loop of line, either under or on top of the deck. The drum is sited aft and the line taken forward, around a pulley, and back aft to the other side of the drum. The sheets can then be attached to this loop and both will move identical distances when the drum turns. As long as they are then attached to the booms at the same distance from the boom's pivot points, identical angles of boom will be generated.

R/C box system used on this yacht with everything mounted in the box. Unfortunately the servo and winch are working in hostile conditions. Note lightweight balsa linkage to rudder.

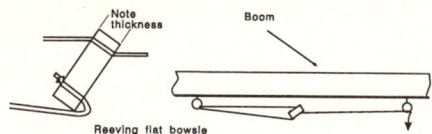

To calculate how far away from the boom pivot point the sheet attachment to the boom can be made, it is first necessary to measure the total movement of sheet allowed by the winch by operating if from full in to full out. The boom pivot point to sheet point length can then be calculated from the formula $\sqrt{\dfrac{L^2}{2}}$ where L is winch travel.

If you have a twin drum winch, it can be fixed almost anywhere along the axis of the model and the sheets attached at any convenient point, making sure that both sails are drawn in or let out together.

However careful one is in measuring and attaching the sheets to the loop, it is almost inevitable that there will be some difference in length between the two. If this is not corrected, the jib and main will let out by different angles, ruining the performance of the sail system. The lengths can be adjusted by small devices called 'bowsies'. These can be either flat or ring type. The former can be cut from 2 mm thick plastic and the holes should only be slightly larger than the cord diameter.

Scale sailing models are quite tricky subjects for R/C, but rewarding when right.
Photo: J. D'Oylywright.

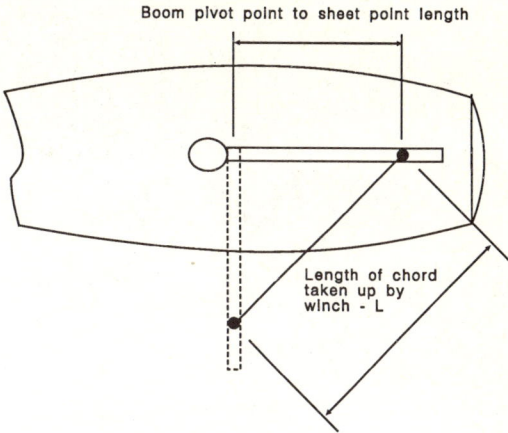

The correct way to thread them is to feed the cord through one end hole, through the required eye and then through the other hole of the bowsie from the same side as the first hole was threaded.

Scale Sailing Systems

R/C of scale sailing craft is particularly difficult because of the number and variety of sails. One system for square sails is to connect the course braces to a sheeting line on deck each side, a winch paying out on one side as it hauls in on the other. The courses are thus braced round fairly simply, and the sails above will follow round if their clews are attached to the yard below. Alternatively, especially where lower and upper topsails, topgallants, and royals may be fitted, their braces may be taken back to the mast behind, turned down the mast through guides, and then from the foot of the mast to the sheeting lines. Or this may be done for one mast only and, where square sails are used on other masts, the yard arms may be connected with lines so that bracing round the yards on, say, the foremast automatically draws the other yards round.

A separate winch is required for fore and aft sails and this can be arranged as for Bermuda rigged yachts as described earlier.

Chapter 5
Speed Control

Microswitches

THE SIMPLEST form of controlling an electric motor is to switch the power supply with microswitches. These can be obtained from the High Street electronics shops and will handle surprisingly large currents for their size,

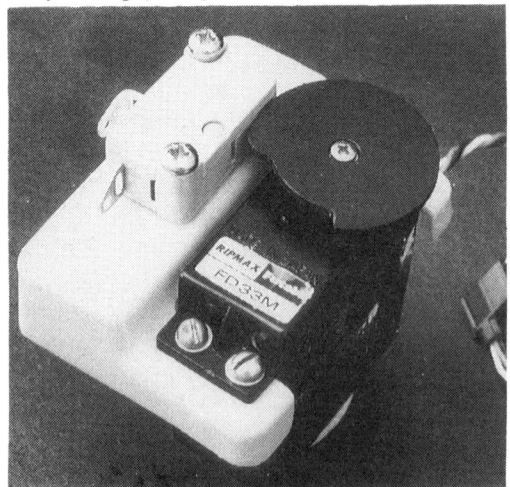

Simple styrene moulding to take servo and microswitch operated by cut away servo disc with cam.

certainly enough to control any scale boat, and most fast electric models. A number of ingenious circuits have been devised using microswitches, ranging from the very basic on/off to circuits giving forward and half speed astern, see diagrams. To operate the micro-switch, this must be mounted on a small bracket fitted to the servo, either by utilising the servo mounting brackets or perhaps with contact adhesive, allowing

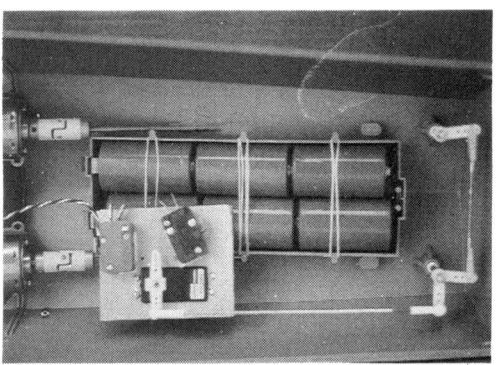

Two microswitches mounted on a simple ply plate fixed to the servo lugs. Note also twin rudder installation linkage.

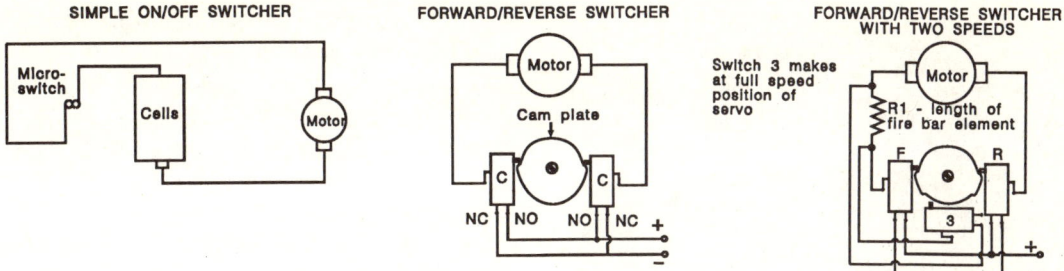

the microswitch lever arm to be operated by the servo disc which needs to be cut into cam shapes. There are also some commercial brackets which fit onto most servos and come complete with pre-shaped cams.

Resistance Boards

If you don't wish to dabble with microswitches and resistors, etc., and it can be a bit of a time-consuming and fiddly exercise, then the resistance wiper board controller may be the answer. An insulated piece of board, about 2" square, has a special resistive foil material fixed to its surface in various shapes and areas over which a wiper arm attached to the servo output arm is rotated. The wiper makes electrical contact with the resistance board and, by means of suitable circuitry, control is achieved in relatively small increments of motor speed. The fineness of control depends on the number of tracks and wipers; a usual number is three to five in forward and astern. Some of the boards can be mounted directly on top of the servo with the output shaft protruding up through the board and with the wiper arm fixed to the output shaft. Others are mounted on a separate board and operated by way of a conventional link from the servo. It is important that the correct rated board is selected to suit the power of the motor. If in doubt, err on the high side as far as the board is concerned.

While these units work very well, and give a reasonably good control, they have some limitations. First of all, they depend on good electrical contact between the wiper and the board and will only operate reliably as long as both surfaces are clean, dry and not worn or corroded. If they do become corroded, don't use glasspaper for cleaning; rub them over with a hard pencil or preferably ink rubber. They are also not so good at very low revs and so some intricate manoeuvres such as docking a model boat are difficult. However, they are very good value for money and, with care, will give good service.

Electronic Speed Controllers

The best method of controlling an electric motor is undoubtedly with an electronic speed controller which takes

Two resistance type wiper boards control each of the two motors in this model.

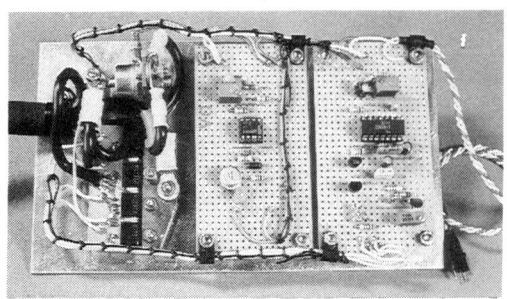

Electronic speed controllers can be home-made – this one from a circuit published in *Radio Control Boat Modeller* magazine. As not all modellers are adept at printed circuit techniques, Veroboard was used which does tend to make for quite a bulky unit, however in most boats this is not a problem. The saving is about 50% on commercial units. *Photo: Ray Brigden.*

the place of a servo and plugs directly into the receiver. A typical unit is about twice the size of a receiver, although they are getting smaller day by day. There are four other wires, two go to the battery and two to the motor.

There has been considerable development in these units over recent years, mainly because of the voracious appetite of the model car fraternity where these controllers are continually asked to switch larger and larger currents, and become physically smaller and lighter.

At the present time, it is possible to buy forward-only controllers for car purposes which will handle 500 amps momentarily and continually run for five minutes at 25 amps or more. Very few boats require this specification, but the advantage is that these units are very robust for boat use, as long as they are kept dry.

All units will be capable of giving fully proportional control from zero revs to maximum, and many have a reduced performance mode in reverse. All these parameters can be set up to suit your model and transmitter by small trim screws on the controller. They are easy to set up, taking only a few minutes. The electronic controller does not work by reducing the voltage, as the resistance controller discussed earlier does, but actually feeds full voltage to the motor in very short bursts. The motor is fooled into thinking it is receiving a continuous current, but will slow down or speed up as the frequency of the pulses fed to it are changed. This gives excellent torque characteristics throughout the entire speed range, with the ability to turn so slowly that you can count the revs!

In a car, the controller is continually cooled by air rushing over it as the car moves. In a boat, the controller will probably be tucked away in a tight and airless situation and will rapidly warm

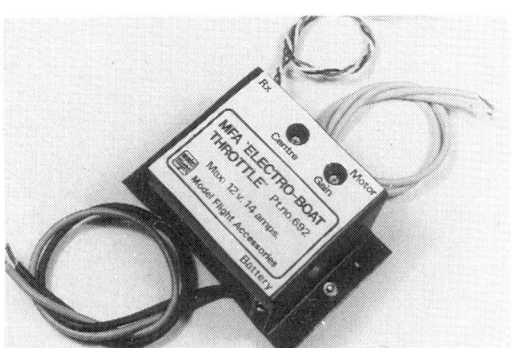

An electronic speed controller with reversing facility. Wire at top right goes to receiver; two light wires to motor and two wires at bottom left to battery. The small pots allow for setting up the motor neutral and full speed to suit the individual system.

Another electronic speed controller, again with reverse. Maximum rating of this unit is 12 volts 10 amps.

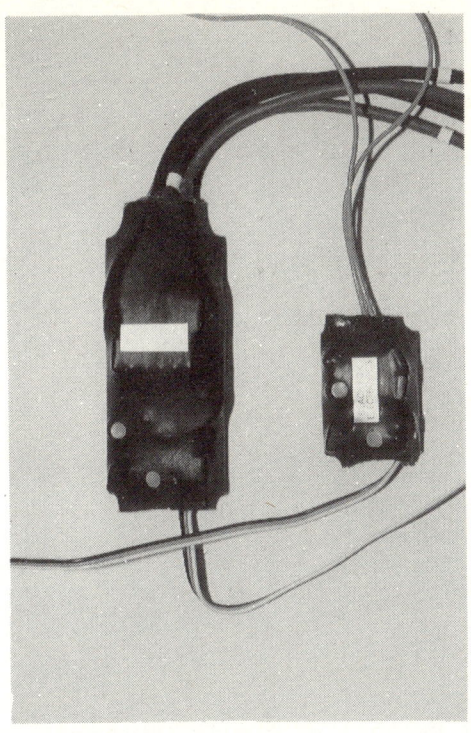

Two high performance speed controllers designed for high currents, around 25 amps continuous at 8.4 volts. The left unit has a reversing relay fitted; the right is forward only. Basically designed for the R/C car market, they can be very suitable for high performance boats, and the larger sports models.

up. They are designed to handle high currents and will run quite hot, and on most small models there will be no problem as the current supplied to the motor will more than likely be well below the specification of the controller. However, if you do note that the controller is hot to the touch after a run, then it might be worthwhile mounting it on a large piece of aluminium plate to act as a heatsink. In a fast electric model, the plate could be watercooled.

Electronic speed controllers are extremely reliable as long as they are not abused and washed! The higher the current rating required, the more expensive they are. If you only intend to operate small to medium-sized scale models, it is a waste of money to buy a high power controller but, if in the future you may want to run fast electrics or even a large-scale model, then go for the high output controller. This will work perfectly well on the smaller models, but the opposite most definitely does not apply.

Finally, make absolutely certain that you follow the wiring instructions properly. It is not difficult but it is easy to make a mistake and wire the battery leads the wrong way round. Some controllers are protected and will not be damaged if you do this, but others are not protected and will be expensively damaged. And, what's more, the manufacturers fit a device which tells them that it has been connected the wrong way round, so it's no good telling them it didn't work out of the box!

Chapter 6
Power Source

Dry Cells

OVER THE YEARS, a wide range of dry cells has been used for R/C gear, but today, almost without exception, there is only one type of battery used, the common 1.5 volt pencell. Most transmitters require eight and most receivers four. At first glance there appears to be little difference between the standard cells and the higher power HP7 type, except that the latter are a little more expensive. A little testing, however, will show that the voltage supplied by the HP cell is higher than the standard; and more importantly, the voltage falls at a slower rate with the HP cell and it has a higher capacity. An additional benefit is that it is leakproof. The alkaline-manganese type of cell (Duracell) is also of 1.5 volts nominal, with a much bigger capacity and even slower rate of drop off. It would obviously be a much better choice, but only if you have a transmitter with a battery voltage display. Otherwise, just in case, one

tends to throw the batteries away long before they are exhausted.

The receiver situation is not so straightforward. Ideally one should replace these before every outing but this is going to be an expensive exercise. Purchasing an electronic voltmeter might be an answer, discarding cells that fall below 1.1 volts after the equipment has been switched on for a minute or two. Also, it is false economy to

A range of batteries. From left to right, alkaline manganese primary cell; standard primary cell; pencell nicad; 9 volt nicad; 1.2 ampere hour nicad; 2.5 ampere hour lead acid gel cell; and, in front, a 1000 size DEAC.

replace just one cell in a pack. The others will rapidly drag it down to their common level.

Nicads

These are rechargeable cells of exactly the same physical dimensions as the dry pencells, but they are based on nickel cadmium, and are known as secondary cells (dry cells are called primary) and have a nominal voltage of 1.2 volts. As the voltage is considerably lower than that for a pencell – for instance eight cells in a transmitter will give a nominal voltage of 12 volts with dry pencells and 9.6 volts with nicads – one is prompted to examine how they can be used as a direct replacement. The answer revolves around current delivery and voltage drop off. Dry pencells start dropping steadily in voltage from the moment they are made, which is why you should buy from a source with a big turnover, whereas nicads, as they are known for short, maintain their voltage almost regardless of current drain until just a few moments before they are exhausted. They are also completely sealed and require no maintenance apart from being kept clean and dry. The only disadvantage is initial cost – some three to four times that of dry cells – plus, of course, a charging device, between £9 and £25, depending on sophistication. So, taking these prices into account, a rechargeable power source plus charger will be paid for after some ten to twelve battery changes with dry cells.

Most receivers require a four cell pack, nominally giving 6 volts. Replacing with nicads is going to drop the voltage to 4.8 volts, but with most receivers this will not cause any problems, for two reasons. The first is the same as for the transmitter situation where nicads maintain their voltage throughout their

entire discharge, and also that most receivers actually drop the voltage to 4.8 volts for their operation.

You may be offered or hear of button cells, manufactured by a West German firm called DEAC. These cells are made in a wide range of capacities. However, the sizes most used are 225, 500 and 1000. The numbers refer to their capacities; the 225 is 0.225 ampere hour – the 500 is therefore equivalent to the pencell in terms of capacity. These rechargeable cells are welded together in any number and provide equivalent battery voltages as follows:

Cells:	2	3	4	5	6	7	8
Voltage:	2.4	3.6	4.8	6.0	7.2	8.4	9.6

They used to be almost universal in transmitter and receiver applications, but have now been almost entirely superceded by pencells. One point to remember is that they are not suitable for fast charging.

Charging

Replacing the dry cells with nicads is the easy bit. You can continue to remove the nicads from the receiver and transmitter battery boxes when they need recharging and you will need some extra battery cases, again available at High Street electronics stores, to hold the nicads while they are charging, so why not let the existing battery box and transmitter case do that job?

The receiver is easy. Most receivers will have been supplied with a battery harness and switch. The simplest method is to solder two lengths of wire, preferably red to the positive and black to the negative, to the terminals of the battery case. The other ends of the two leads should be soldered or connected to a suitably polarised socket. The output leads from the charger are then

Battery boxes for pencells, DEACs and 1.2 ampere hour nicads.

Another way of expressing 0.5 ampere hours is 0.5×1000 or 500 milliamp hour. Theoretically, it would be possible to take 500 milliamps from the battery for 1 hour, or 5 milliamps for $500/5 = 100$ hours, or any combination of current and time which, when multiplied together, produces 500 milliamp hour. This statement must be treated with some caution, however, as the majority of batteries perform best at or near their specified hourly rates, ie. $C/10$ in our example. This characteristic is much more important when using fast charging techniques but, for electronic use, practically the full nominated capacity is available.

Charging times should be as per the manufacturer of the charger's instructions, which will usually be 14 hours at 50 milliamps for pencell size nicads. This is calculated from their capacity of 500 milliamps per hour, which is the amount of electrical energy they can discharge in a specific time. The mathematicians will have worked out that with a 500 milliamp battery, surely if it is charged at 50 milliamps, charging time should be $500/50 = 10$ hours. Quite right, but during the charging process, which is a chemical reaction taking place inside the battery, some heat energy is generated and this has to be provided for, hence the extra four hours.

If you are not going to use your equipment for a long time, it is a good idea to remove the cells, even if you have fitted nicads. Nicads can be stored in a discharged state, but may need a couple of cycles to bring them back into peak form. Indeed, it is now considered good practice occasionally to allow nicads to be completely drained by leaving the transmitter/receiver on until they are absolutely flat, and then giving them a couple of charge/discharge cycles.

wired to a matching plug. The switch in the harness will prevent the changing supply finding its way to the receiver.

A similar principle can be applied to the transmitter, but in this case you will not normally have two terminals that can be reached from the outside of the case. It will be necessary to remove the back of the transmitter case and investigate. The important point is not to connect the charging point after the main power switch – always before. Some transmitters have a suitable blanked-off hole in their plastic casing where the socket can be fixed, otherwise you need to find a suitable spot to drill the necessary hole. Finally, of course, if your equipment is still under warranty, then any dismantling or modifications to the internals will certainly invalidate your guarantee.

Many modellers are confused by the terminology associated with battery capacity. C stands for the total amount of energy which can be obtained from the battery when fully charged. The nominated capacity, for example 0.5 ampere hour, is that which will be obtained when the battery is discharged at such a rate or current as will bring it to a fully discharged state in ten hours, hence $C/10$ or the ten hour rate.

BEC

Electronic speed controllers designed for the model car fraternity, and now some for boats as well, include a controlled electrical feed to the receiver. It is not a very well known fact that the battery feed to a receiver can be through any of the servo sockets and not just the socket reserved for the battery plug. In most instances this has no positive use. However, if the device being controlled can generate the correct voltage for the receiver to work on, this can be fed back down the line to the receiver. The advantage is that the model does not have to carry an extra battery supply for the receiver and this can be important in terms of weight or space saving in very small models.

Beware of the main drive battery dropping in voltage below the 4.8 volts required for the receiver to operate properly, otherwise control will be lost. This is very unlikely in a model boat system though; if it does, you can hardly walk out and recover the model like you can with a car!

Spark Ignition and Electrical Interference

In recent years four stroke engines have become quite popular in model boats, sometimes commercially-made model engines, otherwise converted industrial engines from chain saws. These engines have electrical ignition systems, which can cause interference problems, some times very difficult to track down and isolate. If in doubt, try fitting a metal shield between the engine and R/C system, perhaps by bonding a thin aluminium plate to the most convenient bulkhead. Litho plate is excellent and free supplies are probably available from a local printer if the purpose is explained. Make sure all the engine connections, particularly the HT leads, are secure.

Electrical interference from electric drive motors can also show in many different ways. Symptoms are occasional glitches of steering servo when throttle is operated; intermittent or variable output from an electronic speed controller; or just a general feeling of control not being what it should be. The remedy is straightforward. You need to fit suppressors in the form of tiny capacitors to the motor. These are sometimes available as a pack from the model shop but can also be obtained from the High Street electronics outlet. You need some .01 to .05 microfarad capacitors, one of which is simply soldered across the brush terminals and one each from the brush to a metal part of the motor can. Motors in servos and winches are protected by the manufacturer so you don't need to worry about them.

How Much Sailing?

The answer to this question depends upon the size of the battery pack in terms of capacity, the number of servos in the model, and what type of model. For most power boats, multi-racing, steering, etc., a 500 milliamp hour pack should provide power for at least two hours – assuming that linkages and servo operated controls are free. A binding control will take very large

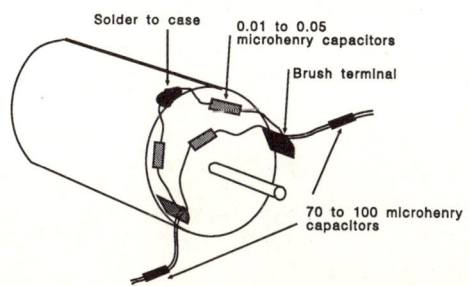

Solder to case
0.01 to 0.05 microhenry capacitors
Brush terminal
70 to 100 microhenry capacitors

currents and reduce operating time dramatically. Most scale models, with their lighter loaded control surfaces, should last slightly longer, but the addition of horns, lights, and operating ancillaries will obviously have a marked effect. However, if one wishes to save weight, very important in fast electrics, a 100 milliamp hour pack will last something like 15 to 20 minutes. At the other extreme, yacht sails controlled by a winch take a relatively large drain, and the fact that most yacht races are longer than those for power boats means it is worthwhile considering a 1000 milliamp hour pack, or even the larger 1.2 ampere hour C size cells.

Simple Problem Solving

If the worst does happen and all systems are no-go, despite all your preparation, don't despair. Modern R/C equipment is very reliable and component failure is extremely rare, unless the gear has been ill-treated. Loss of control is seldom caused by component failure or outside sources such as radio interference. It is much more likely to be the effect of weak or discharged batteries, poor connections, stiff or sloppy linkages, or water ingress.

A suspected failing battery can be checked by a voltmeter with the cells connected and the unit switched on. Replace with new dry cells or freshly-charged nicads. If a servo is suspected as being faulty, simply swap the plugs over at the receiver to check. This will immediately pick out the culprit as servo or receiver. Substitution of a friend's receiver or transmitter will identify problems in those areas, although mixing of different manufacturer's equipment should be avoided. Crystals can stop working, especially if they have been banged around. They are delicate and can easily be damaged, especially by vibration. Also, it is quite easy to bend the legs as they are inserted into the transmitter or receiver and not realise that this has occurred.

Check wires for continuity with a 1.5 volt battery and a torch bulb. Sometimes wiggling a wire will highlight a broken wire hidden by insulation, a common cause of intermittent operation. Check the on/off switch in particular and make sure the contacts are not corroded. Clean with a switch cleaner and replace as soon as possible. Intermittent operation can also be caused by a broken aerial wire, especially at the point where it leaves the receiver.

If still no joy, then carefully pack the equipment and return to the manufacturers or their agents for repair.

Chapter 7
Dos and Don'ts

In this chapter we list some dos and don'ts of radio installation. They are in no particular order so no store should be placed on where they appear in the list. Some have been mentioned in earlier text, some are new; all are important.

DO   join a model club and help yourself to all the free advice so readily available.

DO   decide what type and mode of equipment you want and then shop around for the best value.

DO   plan your installation carefully.

DO   double check everything as you go.

DO   protect R/C equipment against water and vibration.

DO   ensure that connections are not stressed and likely to break or pull apart.

DO   route the receiver aerial wire away from motors, drive batteries, speed controllers.

DO   avoid metal to metal clevises.

DO   ensure that snakes and tubes are adequately supported, and that they are clean and free from oil and dust.

DO   avoid overtensioning closed loop systems. They just need to be slop free.

DO   keep resistance board speed controllers clean and dry.

DO   make a loop on whip aerials to avoid damage to eyes or person.

DO   regularly inspect yacht rigging for chafing and wrinkles in shrouds.

DO   ventilate hull interiors between sailing sessions, and leave hatches off radio boxes. Dry out silica gel packs.

DO   regularly inspect cells for corrosion, especially the negative leads which are prone to electrolytic action.

DO   make a suitable stand for all your models.

DON'T   mix radio equipment from various manufacturers without first obtaining advice. Servos can usually be interchanged, but interchanging transmitters and receivers, particularly FM, is fraught with danger.

DON'T operate your radio equipment for more than five minutes with the aerial retracted. This may cause damage to the output transistor.

DON'T allow clevises to foul output discs.

DON'T allow receivers and battery packs to float around in boxes – pack them with foam or secure with servo tape.

DON'T store radio equipment in damp or hot places.

DON'T switch on until you are sure your frequency is clear. Always fly a frequency flag and use the pegboard if one is in operation.

DON'T forget to take a well-equipped toolbox, complete with tools, spares, batteries, glow-plugs, fuel, starting cord or starter, propellers, elastic bands, instant glues, some means of retrieving the model, oil, towels, crystals, etc.

Appendix
Manufacturers' and
suppliers' addresses

Great Britain

ABCO UK Ltd., 1 Shipton Close, Walshaw Park, Bury, Lancs. BL8 1QH.

ASP Plans Service, Argus House, Boundary Way, Hemel Hempstead, Herts. HP2 7ST.

Amerang Ltd (Billing), Commerce Way, Lancing, West Sussex, BN15 8TE.

Boats and Models, 8 Elm Close, Lingwood, Norwich, Norfolk. NR13 4TQ.

C.E. Systems, 32 Churchill Crescent, Wickham Market, Suffolk, IP13 0RW.

Calder Craft, 8 New Street, Meltham, Huddersfield, West Yorkshire. HD7 3NT.

Chart Micro Mold, Chart House, Station Road, East Preston, Littlehampton, West Sussex, BN16 3AG.

Dean's Marine, The Old School, Main Street, Farcet, Peterborough.

H.F.M. Marine, 158 Queens Road, Clarendon Park, Leicester, LE2 3FS.

Humbrol Ltd., Marfleet, Hull, HU9 5NE.

Irvine Engines Ltd., Unit 2, Brunswick Industrial Park, Brunswick Way, New Southgate, London N11 1JL.

Kingston Mouldings, 411 Ringwood Road, Parkstone, Poole, Dorset, BH12 4LX.

Lesro Models Ltd., Stony Lane, Christchurch, Dorset, BH23 7LQ.

Modeen Steam Driven Models, PO Box 70, Oldham Lancs.

Nylet Ltd., PO Box 7, Fordingbridge, Hants. SP6 1RQ.

Prestwich Model Centre, 8 Warwick Street, Prestwich, Near Manchester.

Racing Models, 1 Melrose Avenue, Whitton, Middlesex.

Ripmax Ltd., Green Street, Enfield, EN3 7SJ.

Sirmar Model Ship Fittings, 7 Old Barn Road, Wordsley, Stourbridge, West Midlands, DY8 5XW.

Stuart Turner Ltd., Henley-on-Thames, Oxon, RG9 2AD.

United States of America

Ace Radio Control Inc., P O Box 511, 116 West 19th Street, Higginsville, MO 64037, USA. Tel: (816) 584 7121

Airtronics Inc., 11 Autry, Irvine, CA 92718, USA.

Du-Bro Products, 480 Bonner Road, Wauconda IL 60084, USA. Tel: (312) 526 2136.

Dumas Products Inc., 909 East 17th Street, Tucson AZ 85719, USA, Tel: (602) 623 3742.

Futaba Corporation of America, 4 Studebaker, Irvine, CA 92718 USA. Tel: (714) 455 9888.

Carl Goldberg Models Inc., 4734 West Chicago Avenue, Chicago, IL 60651, USA.

Hobby Lobby International Inc., 5614 Franklin Pike Circle, Brentwood, TN 37027, USA. Tel: (615) 373 1444.

J & M Products Co., 16301 Philomene, P O Box 214, Allen Park MI 48101, USA. Tel: (313) 381 5589.

J/R Hobby Dynamics Distribution, P O Box 3726, Champaign, IL 61826-3726, USA. Tel: (800) 458 0241.

J'Tec, 164 School Street, Daly City, CA 94014, USA. Tel: (415) 756 3400.

Lindberg Hobbies Inc., 940 North Shore Drive, PO Box 188, Lake Bluff, IL 60044, USA. Tel: (312) 296 6290.

Midwest Products Co. Inc., 400 South Indiana Street, P.O. Box 564, Hobart, IN 46342, USA. Tel: (219) 942 1134.

Minicraft Models Inc., 1510 West 228th Street, Torrance, CA 90501, USA. Tel: (213) 775 8836.

Model Rectifier Corporation (MRC) 200 Carter Drive, Edison NJ 08817, USA. Tel: (201) 248 0400.

Octura Models Inc., 7351 North Hamlin Avenue, Skokie, IL 60076, USA. Tel: (312) 674 7351

Parma International Inc., 13927 Progress Parkway, North Royalton, OH 44133, USA. Tel: (216) 237 8650.

Prather Products Inc., 1660 Ravenna Avenue, Wilmington, CA 90744, USA. Tel: (213) 835 4764.

Sig Manufacturing Co Inc., 401-7 South Front Street, Montezuma, IA 50171, USA. Tel: (515) 623 5154.

Universal Energy R/C Supplies, 130-C East Jefryn Boulevard, Deer Park, NY 11729, USA. Tel: (516) 586 9584.

Two winning magazines for model skippers!

MODEL BOATS

MODEL BOATS is the only full colour magazine for boat modellers, with up to 12 pages of colour each month.

Every issue is packed with full size plans, kit reviews, news from the boat modelling world and invaluable tips on boat building, all in a big, bright and informative package.

In fact, with regular submissions from the two major model boating associations and the country's top two model boat photographers, it is no wonder that MODEL BOATS is the leader in its market.

RADIO CONTROL BOAT MODELLER

RADIO CONTROL BOAT MODELLER has rapidly established a devoted following amongst radio control enthusiasts.

A bi-monthly magazine with an accent on scale yachts and power boats, it brings you regular kit reviews, regatta news from home and abroad, a model yachting column, full size plans and features on both simple and sophisticated electronics.

For both newcomers and established hobbiests alike, there are no better magazines!

SUBSCRIPTION RATES	UK	Europe	Middle East	Far East	Rest of the World
Model Boats – published monthly	£18.00	£22.40	£22.50	£24.20	£22.80
Radio Control Boat Modeller – published bi-monthly	£8.70	£11.30	£11.40	£12.35	£11.55

Airmail Rates on Request

Remittance and delivery details should be sent to:
Subscription Manager **(CG50)** Argus Specialist Publications,
Argus House, Boundary Way, Hemel Hempstead, Herts HP2 7ST